all gone

THINGS THAT AREN'T THERE ANYMORE

by david seidman

General Publishing Group
Los Angeles

Publisher: W. Quay Hays
Editorial Director: Peter L. Hoffman
Editor: Dana Stibor
Art Director: Chitra Sekhar
Front Cover Design: Robert Avellan
Production Director: Trudihope Schlomowitz
Prepress Manager: Bill Castillo
Production Artist: Maritta Tapanainen
Production Assistants: David Chadderdon, Thomas Hultgren, Russel Lockwood, Gaston Moraga, Bill Neary
Proofreaders: Steve Baeck, Amy Castor

For information:
General Publishing Group, Inc.
2701 Ocean Park Boulevard, Suite 140
Santa Monica, CA 90405

Library of Congress Cataloging-in-Publication Data

Seidman, David, 1958-
    All gone : things that aren't there anymore / by David Seidman.
      p. cm.
    ISBN 1-57544-041-5
      1. United States—Social life and customs—1971- —Miscellanea.
2. United States—Social life and customs—1971- —Pictorial works.
3. Popular culture—United States—History—20th century—Pictorial
works. 4. Popular culture—United States—History—20th century-
-Miscellanea.   I. Title.
E169.02.S435   1998
306'.09'04—dc21   98-21600
                                               CIP

Printed in the USA by RR Donnelley & Sons Company
10 9 8 7 6 5 4 3 2 1

General Publishing Group
Los Angeles

table of contents

acknowledgments

No one writes a book like this alone.

I owe my deepest thanks to the hardworking and imaginative crews at the photo services that supplied this book's pictures: Jemal Creary of FPG International, Norman Currie of Corbis-Bettmann, Mike Eby of Allsport Photography, Chris Nichols of Shooting Star, Jason Pagan of Black Star, Allen Reuben of Culver Pictures, Michael Shulman of Archive Photos, and Linda Ritter of Brown Brothers. And a special thanks to Sam Baxter, who took pictures especially for this book.

My researchers were invaluable. My thanks to all of them. They came through fast and reliably, and I appreciate their work deeply: Chuck Bednar, Marc Dupee, Dorian Frankel, Bruce Gordon, Marj Jokisch, Maureen Haggerty, Keith Kellett, Julie Lesser, and Bruce Sterling and the Dead Media Working Group.

Several companies and other organizations graciously provided information about their now-defunct products. Special thanks to Megaera Ausman of the United States Postal Service, Joanne Costa of Pfizer, Vicki Cwiok of Sears, Brian Daly of Unisys, Mark Dollins of Quaker Oats Company, Sara Eliasen of Raytheon, Ken Goff of American Safety Razor, Dr. Sheldon Hocheiser of AT&T, Myron Holtzman of Anheiser-Bush, Karen Kofer of Kellogg, Beth McElhinney of Apple Computer, Rita McKay of Chrysler Corporation, Michael McKenna of Lucent Technologies, Patrick Morris of Binney & Smith, William O'Dea of Keuffel & Esser Company, Whitney Said of Ford Motor Company, Lee Saegesser of NASA, Donna Thede of Kellogg, and Ellen Zimny of The Coca-Cola Company.

In a project like this, the poor writer depends on libraries. I am deeply grateful to the following: Beverly Hills Public Library (particularly the periodicals room staff); L.A. County's West Hollywood branch library; Los Angeles Public Library's central library and Robertson branch library; Santa Monica Public Library's main library; UCLA's College Library, University Research Library, Biomedical Library, and Music Library; and USC's Doheny Library.

This book wouldn't exist if GPG's Peter Hoffman and Quay Hays hadn't called me in to write it. I am also grateful to my editor, Dana Stibor, the book's designer, Chitra Sekhar, and the designer of the front cover, Robert Avellan. As always, I appreciate the work of my attorney, Paul S. Levine, who negotiated my contract to write the book. Special thanks are due to photographer Michi Sherwood, who actually made me look good (a challenging task, I assure you). I am also grateful to my family, especially Marvin and Phyliss Seidman, for offering so much warmth and support.

Thanks to one and all.

David Seidman
West Hollywood, California
1998

dedication

To

Andy Conchelos

Rachel Seidman

Tony Conchelos

Eric Seidman

These are some of the things

that your parents and grandparents are talking about

when you don't know what they're talking about.

foreword
The Silly Century

We 20th Centuryites are silly. We exchange one style of clothes for the next, blow up old buildings to make room for new ones, junk workable technology when fresh gadgets come along, and then wax gooey about the Good Old Days. If the Good Old Days were all that good, why'd we dump them in the first place?

That's part of what this book is about. Being a 20th Centuryite, I find myself wondering whatever happened to a brand of toy that I had as a kid or a building that I've seen in old movies. So when Peter Hoffman, editorial director of General Publishing Group, called me in to discuss writing this book, I leaped at it.

So why *did* we trash so many things that at one time we loved? For that matter, how did they come into existence in the first place? Were they really all that popular, or does the golden glaze of sentimental memory make them seem better than they really were?

Take enclosed phone booths. So secure and private were these mini-rooms that Superman changed clothes in them. They were genuinely omnipresent. But vandals attacked the booths, and advocates for the handicapped protested that they were awkward for wheelchairs, so the Bell System began eliminating them.

Other items vanished simply because people lost interest in them. One of the most famous images of chic elegance is that of Audrey Hepburn from *Breakfast at Tiffany's*, biting a long cigarette holder. The thin reed was a sign of the sophisticated lady (although sophisticated men such as Cary Grant sometimes posed with them). Starting in the late 1950s, working-class heroes such as Elvis Presley, Marlon Brando, James Dean, Joan Baez, Janis Joplin, and Bob Dylan didn't bother with such affectations. Although the cigarette holder tried a comeback in the neo-lounge culture of the 1990s, cigarette smoking had declined to the point that long holders couldn't take root as deeply as they had in earlier decades.

And so it goes.

But as I looked into these subjects, I found myself venturing into unexpected areas. Even though the book is called *All Gone: Things That Aren't There Anymore*, I pondered whether I could include types of people who aren't there, like hippies. Although this is a nostalgia book, could I include things that are gone but that people aren't really nostalgic about, like the Soviet Union? I decided to explore it all.

So this isn't just a book of cool pictures and "Aw, remember that?" It is (if you'll let me get highfalutin for a moment) a set of parables about popularity, fables that happen to be factual.

It also, I think, is fun. I certainly had fun working on it, because I kept discovering things that I'd never imagined. I didn't know that Civil War veterans were still alive and active well into the 1950s. I didn't know that the publisher of *Look* magazine got financial backing from his harshest nemesis, the publisher of *Life*. I didn't know that the Motion Picture Production Code, which censored movies for 30 years, originally didn't control the movies but did control the private lives of the sex-mad stars. I didn't know that the inventor of the zoot suit was buried in one—a lavender one, at that.

If you just want to look at the pictures, that's fine, too. That's how my niece and nephews, the ones to whom I dedicate the book, will most likely enjoy it.

So let's get into it. Have fun!

David Seidman
West Hollywood, California
1998

all gone

Chapter One
AROUND THE HOUSE

Housekeeping is immortal. Washing clothes, decorating, cleaning—these are constants of human history.

"We can toss these off in a hurry!"

Sure they can! That's break-resistant dinnerware molded of Melmac

Here's the dinnerware that youngsters *and* parents can treat ever so casually. Smart and colorful, it's molded of MELMAC plastic and is unbelievably resistant to breaking, cracking and chipping.

Furthermore, MELMAC dinnerware is light, easy to stack, quiet in use and washes beautifully in dishpan or machine.

Ask to see this modern dinnerware at your favorite store. If it is not available there now, write to American Cyanamid Company, Plastics Department, 30 Rockefeller Plaza, New York 20, N. Y.

MELMAC dinnerware identified with this insignia complies with the high standards of quality established for heavy-duty melamine dinnerware by industry through the U. S. Dept. of Commerce.

For more about MELMAC turn to page 168

MELMAC dinnerware is available in a wide variety of colors and designs (here are three)...all smart to get, smart to give, smart to use.

The joys of Melmac.

But while the chores and pleasures remain the same, the techniques of housekeeping don't. Take the matter of socks. Kids have always torn holes in their stockings, and yesterday's housewife might have darned the socks; but today's parent simply buys new ones, because he or she has no time for darning and because modern synthetic fabrics have made new socks more affordable. And every parent since prehistory has shouted the kids to dinner, but houses no longer use speaking tubes to carry the shout from room to room.

It's true of other items, too. Getting rid of bugs is an immortal house-keeping problem, but sprays and electric bug-zappers have replaced old-fashioned flypaper. Every family needs dishes, but dishes of Melmac (a trade name for lightweight, easily cleaned melamine plastic) aren't as common as they used to be, reportedly because they soften when microwaved. And every householder wants a handsome home, but how many decorate it with shag carpets or a Negro lawn jockey? (Actually, lawn jockeys are still around, except that their faces are usually painted white.)

And so it goes. Kids will always raid the kitchen and argue that their siblings spend too much time in the bathroom—even as kitchen appliances and aspects of bathroom plumbing vanish and are replaced by new ones.

Pull-chain toilets

Where would we be without the toilet? "That essential convenience of modern living, the flush toilet, was enjoyed by Minoan royalty 4,000 years ago and by few others for the next 35 centuries," writes historian Charles Panati in *Extraordinary Origins of Everyday Things*. "One version was installed for Queen Elizabeth in 1596, devised by a courtier from Bath who was the queen's godson, Sir John Harrington.... [His design] included a high water tower on top of the main housing, a hand-operated tap that permitted water to flow into a tank, and a valve that released sewage into a nearby cesspool."

Pretty close to the classic pull-chain toilet, with its tank above the rest of the device, but the real article didn't exist until the mid-1800s. The prophetically named Thomas Crapper, an English plumber, developed the waste-water preventer, "the very same siphonic cistern with uphill flow and automatic shut-off found in modern toilet tanks," says Kathleen Meyer, author of *How to Shit in the Woods*.

A pull-chain toilet, ready for the next customer.

Around 1900, New Englanders Robert Frame and Charles Neff introduced a ceramic or cast-iron tank, filled with water, that sat high above the squatter's head. (In some homes, the water entered the tank from a storage tank in the attic.) A chain hung from the tank, with a handle at the chain's bottom. In fancy homes, the chain was made of brass and the handle—called the pull—was ivory.

When the squatter pulled the handle, he released the tank's water. It fell through a pipe, ran into the bowl, and washed the squatter's waste away. This set-up became standard in the Western world. Manufacturers made new pull-chain toilets until well into the 20th century.

Soon, though, more homes got their water from municipal pipes in the ground than from storage tanks in the attic. A new toilet came along, with the tank riding not over the squatter's head but just behind him, fairly close to the floor. Flushing this toilet propelled water into the bowl with power to rival that of the high tank and its pipe-enclosed waterfall.

Virtually all toilet makers switched to the new design. Still, the pull-chain toilet provided comfort, convenience, and cleanliness for decades. It allowed every-man the same treatment as royalty. For that, it deserves respect and, yes, even a bit of nostalgia.

Iceboxes

"One of the most frequently seen vehicles on the street in the summertime used to be the ice wagon," writes historian Everett Wilson in his book *Vanishing Americana*. "The ice wagon was usually driven by a husky individual, who also had to cut and weigh the ice and carry it, by means of ice tongs, to the icebox."

Getting some ice into the box.

Ah, the icebox. It stood in nearly every kitchen, often short enough so that the family could lay objects on its flat top. Like today's refrigerator, it had chambers for different foods. Unlike today's fridge, it had a drip pan to collect the melted ice. And better than today's massive fridges, iceboxes often had casters under their legs so that they could be moved.

For kids, the icebox experience was a delight. "On hot days, swarms of young boys followed the ice wagon from house to house and eagerly grabbed the chips of ice which fell from the scales when the iceman weighted and split the large cakes of ice. Sucking these chips helped keep the youngsters cool on hot days," writes author Ishbel Ross in her book *Taste in America*.

But a competitor was looming. "The electric refrigerator...came on the market around 1913," Ross says. It cost a lavish $900 when first introduced and remained a luxury through the 1920s. But in the 1930s, the low-priced Sears Coldspot made refrigeration affordable. "By 1945," says Ross, "the icebox, with its old drip pan, had given way to the electric refrigerator."

True, the convenience of the fridge made household life easier. But more than one small boy, now grown into a venerable grandfather, still remembers with delight the thrill of grabbing the ice chips and slipping them into his mouth on a blazing afternoon.

Washboards

A river and a rock—that was the first washing machine. As water rushed through a piece of fabric, the launderer would literally whack the dirt out. And so laundry day stayed until an unknown inventor created the washboard.

It was simple: a long plank with horizontal ridges, plus a slat at the top to hold a cake of soap. The launderer (or more often, the laundress) immersed board and clothes in a tub of hot, soapy water and rubbed the clothes up and down the ridges, forcing the water and suds through the fibers and, like the rock and river, pushing grime out.

Washboarding was literally a pain. The friction of rubbing, plus constant immersion in hot, soapy water, hurt the laundress' hands. "There was no surer way of developing a strong back and strong arms than by using a washboard regularly," says historian Everett Wilson. If a family prospered, one of its first luxuries was often to hire a laundress.

Scrubbing clothes on a washboard could wear holes in all but the toughest fabrics. Some clothes couldn't take it at all. In the 1941 book *The Way We Wash Our Clothes*, author Eleanor Ahearn advised that laundresses never rub woolens on a board.

Meanwhile, inventors worked to improve or eliminate the board. Electric and gasoline-powered wringer washers came along by 1920. A little later, top-loading washing machines were invented. After World War II, they became as common at home as washboards used to be.

The classic board, in its tub.

Boards remained in use here and there. In 1949, New York City declared a "Dry Day," when Manhattanites were to save water by not bathing or washing clothes; some women obeyed by keeping the taps closed and pulling out washboards to clean their clothes in Central Park Lake. In 1958, refugees who fled from the Soviet Union to Germany were photographed washing their clothes on washboards.

The washboard survived (in the United States, at least) only in music. In 1940, country bluesman Washboard Sam was popular for his "percussive scraping" (as author Francis Davis puts it in *The History of the Blues*). Even now, bands striving for an old-fashioned sound sometimes pull out the old washboard.

Philco home electronics

Philco was huge, on a par with RCA and General Electric. Its fate shows how even the strongest firm can suffer.

The Helios Electric Company was founded in Philadelphia during 1892 to make batteries. Renamed Philco, it moved into radio manufacturing in the 1920s and became a kingpin of the business. The company also made or would soon make car batteries, telephones, air conditioners, washing machines, dishwashers, oven ranges, and other appliances. And it pioneered in television; in 1931, Philco hired Philo Farnsworth, one of TV's inventors, to establish a research laboratory and TV station.

RCA, developing its own TV systems, didn't want anyone creating competing systems. RCA also owned a lot of radio technology, which it licensed to Philco and other radio makers. RCA allegedly told Philco, "If you do business with Farnsworth, you can't do business with RCA." For whatever reason, Philco fired Farnsworth.

Philco soon slowed its TV development even further; its executives felt that TV would cut into its lucrative radio revenue. Besides, says Jeff Kisseloff (author of *The Box: An Oral History of Television, 1920–1961*), "[they] worried that when television did come, RCA would dominate the market." Philco even tried to get the Federal Communications Commission to hinder TV development; but RCA went ahead on its own, leaving Philco further behind.

Eventually, Philco did become strong in TV-set sales. It also made radar equipment, microwave communications, semiconductors (a key part of transistors), missile-guidance systems, and orbital satellites. In 1953, the company hit a peak in profits: $18.2 million. Plus, Philco hired brilliant minds in the new field of computers.

But Philco didn't want truly advanced computer research, just as it hadn't wanted TV. One innovator, Robert Noyce, quit and later founded the computer giant Intel. Another, Gordon Bell, was offered a Philco job but instead went to MIT and Digital Equipment, where he made some of the first office minicomputers.

The Philco Baby Grand, a steal at $49.50.

By the early '60s, Philco's home appliance and electronics sales were off. A legal wrangle (against RCA) over color TV had kept it from selling color sets until years after other companies were in the market.

In 1961, Ford Motor Company bought Philco, mostly for its military and space technology. Philco-Ford (its new name) stopped making ranges, dishwashers, home laundry equipment, air conditioners, radios, and stereo components.

In 1974, Ford sold Philco to GTE-Sylvania, which sold it to the electronics giant Philips. The Philco name vanished from American stores.

Philco wasn't the little company that could. It was the big company that could have—for example, it could have pioneered in computers—but, alas, didn't.

NOT QUITE GONE, BUT MIGHTY SCARCE
Laundry wringers

Push a wet, soapy garment between two pressed-together cylinders, turn a crank, and watch the cylinders squeeze the water out of the cloth and drip into a tub. The shirt or pants that went in dirty and wet come out clean, nearly dry, and ready to hang on the wash line. That was the simple, effective process behind the laundry wringer.

No one knows where the wringer came from. Historian Charles Panati's *Extraordinary Origins of Everyday Things* says that around 1800, launderers used a dolly, "a device resembling an upside-down milkmaid's stool, which fitted into a tub and pummeled clothes, squeezing water out." The basic principle was there, but the two-roller setup wasn't.

Whatever its origin, the wringer was common by 1900. "The wringer generally was mounted on the edge of a laundry tub," notes historian Everett Wilson. "The boy of the family often was pressed into service to turn the wringer on washday and had to be careful because a careless lad would sometimes get his fingers caught in the rollers."

In the early 1900s, the wringer went electric. Speed Queen, Maytag, and other manufacturers' powered wringer washers brought relief to anyone who was turning a crank. For homes without electricity, Maytag, in 1915, introduced gasoline-powered machines—which, the company brags, "were so successful that by 1916, more than 12,000 had been sold.... Within six months of the [machine's] introduction, sales and

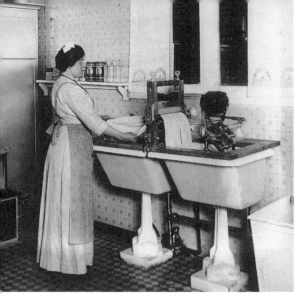

**Wringing it out the
old-fashioned way.**

all gone

production of washing machines doubled." In 1948, Maytag hit an apex of production, making about 2,000 wringers per day.

But starting in the late 1920s, new inventions came in, encroaching on the wringer's turf. The top-loading washer and automatic electric dryer made washing easier than the wringer did.

In 1983, the company that had made nearly 12 million wringer washers quit. "We're experiencing a great sense of loss here," a Maytag executive told *Time* magazine. "The wringer was our only product for 42 years." Speed Queen followed, producing its last wringer washer in 1988.

Wringers didn't vanish entirely. "Wringer washers are still sold in a handful of developing countries, as well as in countries where water is at a premium," notes a Speed Queen report. Middle Eastern nations seem to be the wringer's last outpost.

So if your son asks you, "Dad, what did you mean, 'The boss put me through the wringer'?" you may end up saying, "Well, they've got this machine in Saudi Arabia..."

14

all gone

Chapter Two

CARS

So many cars have come and gone. Where is the Yugo today? Or the Chevrolet Geo? Or the Hispano-Suiza? Whatever happened to the Stanley Steamer, the '57 Chevy, the Chrysler Airflow, the Kaiser-Frazer, the Nash, the Edsel, the LaSalle, the Cord, the Packard, the Hudson?

Some of them were killed by changing times. The Stutz Bearcat, one of America's first luxury performance cars, was beautiful, fast, and popular, but it stayed unchanged while the Duesenberg and other machines outperformed it.

The cars that aren't there anymore could form a book in themselves. They all have their fans; car lovers are a devoted bunch. Some of the lost vehicles even come back, such as the beloved Volkswagen Beetle.

The ones listed below are among the most famous of the old cars.

LUXURY AND PERFORMANCE CARS

Pierce-Arrow

For people at the top of their professions in the late 1920s and early 1930s, the Pierce-Arrow was the car to buy. The Emperor of Japan owned one. So did Adolf Zukor, chairman of Paramount Pictures and the leading movie mogul of the time. The normally frugal Zukor explained this extravagance—a Pierce-Arrow cost upwards of $4,000, while a few hundred bucks could buy a Ford—by saying, "If a man surrounds himself with good things, he sets a standard in his own eyes as well as those of others." In other words, owning a P-A could encourage him and those around him to other great achievements.

Owning a Pierce-Arrow was indeed something of an achievement, and not just

PIERCE-ARROW

Simplicity, as *thinking* people know, is the distinguishing mark of quality—the crowning grace of beauty. During twenty-six years Pierce-Arrow has been simplified to the highest point of efficiency in appearance and operation it exemplifies the unaffected charm

ENCLOSED CARS $2495 TO $8000 *at Buffalo, taxes extra* TERMS IF DESIRED

ed with superb performance and genuine economy in cost and maintenance . . . Pierce-Arrow is the chosen car of those who discriminate, who value it for its simple, impressive elegance as well as for its thrilling responsiveness. The Pierce-Arrow Motor

Pierce-Arrow ad, 1927. The subtle approach, putting the car in the background and the supposed world of its drivers at the fore.

because it was costly. The car was built to high standards. Its body was aluminum, uncommon for autos in those days. Its details were exquisite: "It had a beautiful box of tools right on the running board; vases in the back where you could put cut flowers; and, on the cylinders, little brass priming cups into which you squirted gasoline to start the car in cold weather," wrote Everett Greenbaum in the *Saturday Evening Post*, remembering his father's 1926 P-A. Pierce-Arrows performed in endurance races such as the 857-mile Glidden Tour, which it won five times.

But the Depression steadily cut down the number of people who could afford expensive luxuries like the Pierce-Arrow. In 1937, the proud maker of the Japanese Emperor's car went out of business.

That wasn't quite the end of the Pierce-Arrow, though. "After World War II started," auto historian Brooks T. Brierly has written, "the Pierce-Arrow factory inventory was sold for scrap to make munitions. Knowing about the car, a Buffalo newspaper ran the headline PIERCE INVENTORY SOLD FOR MUNITIONS; HIROHITO TO GET PARTS BY AIR."

One doubts that the Emperor appreciated the irony.

Duesenberg

"No car ever made anywhere has matched the Duesenberg for its rare combined qualities of meticulous craftsmanship, enormous power, and great beauty."

—Howard Bedno, *The People's Almanac #2*

Movie stars Mae West, Tyrone Power, Clark Gable, and Gary Cooper owned Duesenbergs. "Few contemporary American cars, despite a lot of intervening engineering, can match Duesenberg for sheer performance: 0 to 100 mph in 17 seconds, 104 mph in second gear, and a top speed of 129 mph with three tons on board," write automobile journalist Louis Steinwedel and former Duesenberg designer J. Herbert Newport in their book *The Duesenberg: The Story of America's Premier Car*.

Indiana bicycle makers Fred and August Duesenberg started building cars around 1900. But the brothers didn't make classics until they met young businessman E.L. Cord, who in the mid-1920s bought Duesenberg Automobile and Motors. Cord announced plans "to offer the world an automobile of undisputed rank—in fact, the finest thing on four wheels."

He did. The 1928 Duesenberg Model J "was a visual sensation," wrote auto historian Brock Yates. "A long, gaudy collection of sensuous lines, beginning with a bold, upright radiator and culminating—nearly 20 feet later—with a curvaceous tail."

But the masterpiece came in 1932 with the Model SJ. The 320-horsepower SJ made Duesenberg "the most prestigious car in the world," Bedno says. "European royalty, formerly accustomed to English Rolls-Royces and German Daimlers, actually bought American cars."

"The SJ ranks in the minds of many experts as the best automobile ever created," says Yates. It was, he adds, "the fastest production car in existence." And luxurious: "The coachbuilders ransacked the world for the best silk, patent leather, ivory, silver, morocco, pigskin, and prime wood fittings," says Bedno. This beauty and power came at a price. Duesenbergs cost up to $50,000—as much as a sizable house in those days.

The Depression killed the Duesenberg. Few people wanted to spend so much on so gaudy a machine. And, as Bedno explains, "So much money went into making [Duesenberg's] precision machines that expenses often exceeded sales." "By mid-1937, the [Duesenberg] empire plunged into receivership," reports Yates.

In 1947 and 1966, automakers tried to revive the Duesenberg, but they couldn't match the originals' grandeur and prestige. The Duesenberg lives on as a legend and a phrase still used to describe something wildly impressive: "It's a doozy!"

Cadillac Eldorado convertible

It was the luxury monster, a big-finned, long-lined, top-down egomobile. Nothing else seemed so suited to bright pink paint, leopard-print seats, and leather everything else.

Cadillac already had a reputation for opulence and even big fins by 1953, when it introduced the Eldorado. The company promoted it as a "dream car," and it was. Even the price was stunning: $7,750, when the average American household's annual income was $5,410 (according to *Historical Statistics of the United States*).

"The Eldorado convertible received prominent attention when it was used as President Eisenhower's official inauguration parade car in January 1953," write LeRoi Smith and Tony Hossain in *Classic Cars: Cadillac*. "With its imposing price tag, it remained a very exclusive piece of machinery. Only 532 were built."

Demand was high. "In 1954, there was no better status symbol than a red Cadillac convertible," Smith and Hossain say. The 1957 Eldorado Brougham included a vanity case, lipstick, and gold cups on its dashboard. But the greatest was the 1959 model.

"Nothing sums up the optimism of the 1950s better than the 1959 Cadillac convertible," says designer Michael Tambini, author of the design tome *The Look of the Century*, who calls the '59 "the most flamboyant and extravagant of mass-produced cars." He adds, "The tail fins rise over a yard above the ground.... At 20 feet in length and two tons in weight, the Cadillac was unchallenged in size and power.... The steel-framed wraparound windshield recalls the styling of a fighter jet." (Rightly so, since the car's stylist, Harley Earl, admired Clarence Johnson, who designed the Lockheed P-38 fighter.) Journalist C. Van Tune, writing in *Motor Trend*, calls the '59 Eldorado "the definitive '50s icon."

The '50s were soon over. Smaller cars, like the economical Volkswagen Beetle and hot-rodding Chevrolet Corvette, attracted car buyers. In 1965, sales of convertibles started falling.

In 1972, Richard Nixon gave Leonid Brezhnev an Eldorado. Instead of restoring the car to prestige, the gift helped to cement the car's reputation as an indulgence for the old-fashioned. During the gasoline shortages and economic recessions of the 1970s, many Americans viewed the costly, gas-guzzling Eldorado as wasteful and tasteless.

In 1976, the Eldorado was the only American convertible in production. Then Cadillac ceased making them. Six years passed before an American car maker sold new convertibles; they were Chryslers, not Cadillacs.

These days, when a writer or filmmaker wants to summon up the late '50s, he or she's likely to whip out an Eldorado. Although out of production, the massive, flashy, obscene road gobbler is never really gone for long.

Cadillac Eldorado, 1959: practically bulging with self-indulgence.

DeLorean cars

"You built a time machine—in a DeLorean?"

With that incredulous question, Michael J. Fox got laughs nationwide. By the time *Back to the Future* hit movie houses in 1985, the DeLorean Motor Corporation had gone from nothingness to international fame to a joke.

John Zachary DeLorean, a young engineer from Detroit's blue-collar east side, was running Packard Motor Car Company's research and development division by age 30. He moved to General Motors, took over the Pontiac division, and rose to run all of GM's North American truck and car building. He publicly compared himself to Jesus Christ.

Bored as a top executive—"I felt I was no longer playing in the field; I was the guy up there in the stands, and I missed the spirit of aggressive competition"—DeLorean quit in the mid-1970s. He envisioned a car to outdo GM's flashy Chevrolet Corvette. His dream "was sleek and racy, with a stainless-steel skin, a corrosion-resistant, glass-reinforced glass underbody, a 130-hp Renault engine, and gull-wing swing-up doors borrowed from the 1954 Mercedes coupe," wrote *Time* magazine's John DeMott.

DeLorean began raising money. "At least 345 car dealers chipped in a total of $8.6 million," says DeMott. "Other believers were talk-show host Johnny Carson, who kicked in $500,000, and entertainer Sammy Davis Jr., who invested $150,000." An even bigger investor was England. "The British government, which was looking for ways to provide jobs for desperately unemployed workers in Northern Ireland, poured $156 million in grants, loans, and equity capital into the deal. In return, DeLorean built a factory near Belfast that at one time employed 2,600 workers."

DeLorean launched his car in 1981, but few buyers wanted it. The machine cost almost 50 percent more than the Corvette. And while DeLorean planned, financed, and built his car, other car makers continued to innovate, making DeLorean's vision none too special when it finally appeared in showrooms. Moreover, DeLorean's mammoth confidence led him to build too many cars, stretching his expenses too far.

To raise money, DeLorean got involved in cocaine trafficking. But in late 1982, FBI agents posing as drug dealers arrested DeLorean. The British government shut his factory. After less than three years of auto making, the DeLorean Motor Company was out of business.

The low demand for DeLoreans makes them hard to find. To see John DeLorean's dream, rent the *Back to the Future* movies. They're about the surprises that pop up when you invent a new machine.

CARS FOR EVERYONE
Model T Ford

For speed, luxury, beauty, or other prestigious attributes, buy something else. But for a good vehicle at a low price, the only car for millions of drivers was the Model T. The original Tin Lizzie (a misnomer; it was actually made of vanadium steel) simply redefined automobiles.

Before the Model T, autos were rich men's toys. While other cars cost up to $2,800, Henry Ford priced the first Model T, in 1908, at $850—and the price dropped until, in 1923, it hit a rock-bottom $290, or $5 a week on installments. (A 1923 Rolls-Royce cost a fat $10,900.) Anyone making a living could afford a Model T.

The Model T wasn't just inexpensive; it was perfect for its potential customers. In 1908, about half of all Americans lived on farms or in small towns. Ford had grown up on a farm himself, and his car fit rural people snugly. The 20-horsepower Model T could outperform a team of real horses. It was easy to drive and repair; a good thing, as a Model T was the first car for millions. It could handle muddy paths, pull out of holes, act as a tractor, and even (with some modifications) churn butter, grind flour, or saw wood.

Over the nearly 20 years that the Model T was in production, Ford sold more than 15 million. Aviator Charles Lindbergh, ballplayer Babe Ruth, novelist Sinclair Lewis, and the notorious bandit Pancho Villa owned Model Ts. By 1919, at least half of all the cars in the world, and more than half of the cars in America, were Model Ts.

The demand forced Ford, in 1913, to build Model Ts on an assembly line. He didn't invent the concept, but he refined it to near perfection. Before assembly lines, building a Model T took more than 12 hours; in 1920, Ford could produce one per minute. The assembly line became almost every manufacturer's standard means of making cars.

While practical matters such as assembly lines interested Ford, aesthetics didn't. He offered the Model T only in black, because black paint dried faster than other colors and kept his assembly line moving. He never changed the car's style or design.

General Motors chief Alfred Sloan thought differently. As Americans enjoyed the faddishness, freewheeling prosperity, and sheer self-indulgence of the 1920s, Sloan realized that they wanted flash, elegance, and luxury. He gave it to them. The Model T looked fusty by comparison.

In 1927, Ford canceled the Model T, replacing it with the slightly fancier Model A. The Model Ts already on the road didn't vanish—they were durable enough to keep running for years—but eventually, they became museum pieces.

The original better idea: Model T Ford.

Not every museum piece changes the world. The Model T did, and historians will never forget it.

Studebaker

A car salesman meets two customers. One customer says, "We want an automobile that says it all about the new American solidarity—everyone cutting down, doing without, pulling together, generally recreating all the magic of World War II!" The salesman buries his face in his hands as the customer asks, "Say, you don't have any Studebakers, do you?"

Doonesbury's Garry Trudeau wrote that exchange in 1974. He was right; the Studebaker has a glorious past.

It extends to 1852, when brothers John, Henry, Jacob, Clement, and Peter Studebaker formed a blacksmith and wagon-building business. By 1900, the Studebaker Corporation was the world's largest wagon maker.

The company produced its first auto in 1901. "By 1912," writes historian Donald T. Critchlow in *Studebaker: The Life and Death of an American Corporation*, "half of the cars manufactured bore the name plants of [only] seven producers." One of them was Studebaker.

Soon, Studebaker's plant in South Bend, Indiana, covered 121 acres. The company added four factories in Detroit. By 1928, more than 3,800 dealers sold Studebakers.

In 1929, Studebaker's President model set "scores of racing and durability records," says Critchlow. Its Champion was "an immediate hit with the public. Within the first year (1939) over 72,000 Champions were sold." He adds, "By the close of 1939…Studebaker was the largest of the independent [car makers]." World War II defense contracts and the postwar hunger for new cars enriched the company even further.

Then the Big Three automakers began to squeeze the independents, as did high labor costs and wrong guesses about America's taste in cars. In 1954, Studebaker merged with another independent, Packard.

For people weary of the mid-'50s' big-finned, heavy cars, Studebaker, in 1959, offered the compact Lark. It was a hit, but not for long. The Big Three made their own compacts.

Studebaker tried again with 1962's racy Avanti. Its exterior was streamlined, while its interior "appears like a time capsule of Sixties flights of fancy," writes *Car and Driver* reviewer Patrick Bedard. "An overhead console centered above the windshield holds switches for lights and fan. More aircraft-like controls, which pivot like throttle levers and operate the heater and defroster, are located on the tunnel. The gauges are straight out of a cockpit, too."

It wasn't enough. Bedard notes, "Only 4,643 production Avantis were built, and too many of those huddled unsold on dealer lots."

In 1969, Studebaker closed but didn't die. "Aficionados have organized the Studebaker Driver Club, a national organization nearly 18,000 strong who gather at various meets across the country," says Critchlow. "Few companies enjoy such enduring romance, love, and devotion."

AMC Rambler

The Rambler wasn't just one of the first and most successful compact cars; it was a symbol of how an independent automaker could gain an advantage over the Big Three.

The Rambler, born in 1950, existed before its maker did. It was a creation not of American Motors but of the independent Nash auto company.

Soon, Ford, General Motors, and Chrysler were killing independents like Nash. The company merged with Hudson, another independent, in 1954. The combined concern was named American Motors Corporation.

AMC chief George Romney "figured out the way to go was not a frontal attack [on the Big Three] but rather to outflank the competition by offering something that they didn't have, a mid-size or intermediate-size car," says Patrick Foster, author of *American Motors: The Last Independent*. Designer Ed Anderson produced a car that was small outside but roomy and comfortable inside. By 1958, the low-priced Rambler was so popular that it propelled AMC to considerable profits.

Things only got better. By 1963, AMC had converted its other models to Ramblers, so that every AMC car was a Rambler. There were Rambler sedans, station wagons, and convertibles. *Motor Trend* magazine named the entire line as Car of the Year. Dealers ordered more than half a million Ramblers, the highest amount in the car's history. And by controlling expenses—"the basic chassis was used for seven model years, saving millions of dollars in tooling costs," says Foster—AMC earned profits of almost $38 million.

By 1964, though, Romney and Anderson had left AMC. The new management launched a Rambler "muscle car," nicknamed the Scrambler. While the first Rambler was unlike the Big Three's cars, the Scrambler competed straight on against the giants' Mustangs, Camaros, and Cougars. AMC redid its older Ramblers as well.

"To compete in the annual restyling game was a sucker's bet that could only be lost," says Foster. "A small company like AMC would quickly go broke trying to match tooling dollars with the Big Three."

The result was predictable. Foster writes, "On June 30, 1969, the last Rambler ever to be built in America came down the final assembly line." The company had built slightly more than four million Ramblers.

Ford Pinto

The Pinto began as one of America's most promising cars and ended as a deathtrap.

all gone

It was the late 1960s. "Led by the quirky VW Beetle, import [car] sales had climbed steadily, and accounted for 15% of the total U.S. market by 1970," according to *Ford: 1903 to 1984*, by *Consumer Guide* auto editors David Lewis, Mike McCarville, and Lorin Sorensen. "That chunk was too large for Detroit to ignore."

Ford Motor Company executive Lee Iacocca developed a new subcompact: the Pinto, Ford's smallest car ever. It came out on September 11, 1970, about the same time as Chevrolet's similar Vega. But as *Road & Track* magazine reported, "Pinto happens to be the more pleasant car to drive in everyday use…and carries a price tag some $172 less." The Pinto sold for around $2,000.

The Pinto outsold the Vega. In its first year, Ford sold more than 350,000 Pintos, "despite a recall to fix carburetors," says *Ford: 1903 to 1984*, "because of a rash of underhood fires"—a hint of trouble to come.

When Pintos got rear-ended, their gas tanks often blew up. During the car's development, an internal memo "estimated that 180 people could die as a result of the Pinto's defects during the life span of the car, and another 180 could be severely burned," report biographers Peter Collier and David Horowitz in *The Fords: An American Epic*. "These deaths and injuries, the [memo] calculated, had potential 'social costs' of $49.5 million, compared to the $137 million it would cost to fix the Pinto immediately. Thus the modification would not be cost effective." Simply put, Iacocca was so bent on making a cheap car that he skimped on safety.

Pinto's popularity—the company sold 544,208 in the 1974 model year alone—made explosions all the more likely. About 900 people died in Pinto fireballs. One of them was a woman named Lily Gray; in the same accident, 13-year-old Richard Grimshaw suffered burns on 90 percent of his body. In the ensuing lawsuit, the jury fined Ford $124.6 million in punitive damages "so that Ford wouldn't design cars that way again," the jury foreman said.

Ford's stockholders sued as well, partly because they felt that the lawsuit and bad publicity were evidence of mismanagement. And the company fired Iacocca.

Ford stopped making Pintos at the end of the 1980 model year, replacing them with the new Escort. The foreign cars that the Pinto was built to eliminate remain on the road.

AUTO EQUIPMENT AND SUPPLIES
Leaded gasoline

Oil refiners used to throw gasoline away. It was an unwanted by-product in the process of refining kerosene, which lit and heated homes. But by World War I, everyone wanted a car, and gasoline became big business.

Gas worked well in cars because it burned easily. Too easily: in a car's internal-combustion engine, gasoline molecules can ignite before they're supposed to, causing knocking and pinging sounds in the engine.

To prevent this nuisance, gasoline companies added a chemical called tetraethyllead, starting in the 1950s. So far, so good—except that cars emitted the lead through the tailpipe and into the air for anyone to breathe. Lead poisoning can cause vomiting, convulsions, and even death.

Under public pressure to remove lead, Congress passed the Clean Air Act of 1970, which gave the Environmental Protection Agency power to phase down or outlaw fuel additives. On February 22, 1972, the EPA ordered gasoline companies to phase lead down. The companies fought back, even suing the EPA; but on June 14, 1976, the Supreme Court upheld the decision. The phase-down began in 1979.

Lead at the pumps.

Meanwhile, Congress ordered car makers to control emissions. The companies came up with the catalytic converter, a device that reduced pollutants. By the early '80s, all new cars in the United States had the converters.

Unfortunately for gasoline companies, lead can reduce or ruin a converter's efficiency. Moreover, the EPA declared that starting in 1996, it would ban leaded gas altogether. Faced with these pressures, gasoline companies eliminated lead from their fuel. (Under the circumstances, one might expect knocking and pinging to return, but the companies found formulations of gas to reduce the problem.)

The United States isn't the only nation to outlaw lead. "Countries that have banned leaded gasoline include Austria, Brazil, Canada, Colombia, Slovakia, Sweden, and…Thailand," writes *Oil and Gas Journal* columnist Patrick Crow. In May 1996, the World Bank called for countries that still use lead to phase it out. A couple of months later, the European Union "proposed to phase out leaded gasoline from the market by 2000 in most of its 15 member countries and by 2002 in nations with older auto fleets," Crow reports.

It hasn't been easy for the gasoline companies. As late as 1983, bulletin boards at Ethyl Corporation offices proclaimed LEAD IS NOT DEAD.

Fortunately for lungs, it eventually was.

Running boards and rumble seats

Look at old movies, and you'll see them.

Running boards: A robber's driving from the scene of his crime—but a cop's after him, standing on the running board of a pursuing prowl car and taking aim with his revolver.

Rumble seats: It's a double date in an open car. While some handsome slickster is enjoying the front seat, his left hand on the wheel and right arm around a pretty girl, teenage Andy Hardy (or an equivalent) is in the tight rumble seat in back, crammed next to a homely girl who won't shut up. A rain starts, and the Romeo up front pulls the top up to protect himself and his lady, while Andy gets soaked.

The first cars didn't have rumble seats or running boards. They didn't even have doors. But by 1905, automakers were installing side doors, which gave women a problem.

Back then, a car's tires protruded beyond its body. A woman had to lift her leg up and past the width of the tire to enter the car, an awkward job in the full, heavy skirts of the day. Hence the running board—literally a board running between the front and back tires—which turned one long step into two small ones.

Rumble seats and running boards often came together. Ford's 1932 V8 Roadster, for example, had both of them; so did models from Packard and other automakers.

As the years rolled on, however, rumble seats vanished, replaced by full-scale back seats or nothing at all. Running boards disappeared, too. New cars tucked the tires inside the car's body, making an unbroken, aerodynamically smooth sweep from front to back. A lady could enter a car more easily, with no need for a running board.

Running boards did persist, but primarily in vans, trucks, sport utility vehicles, and old-style Volkswagen Beetles. "The new vans, which are high off the ground, make it difficult for senior citizens and children to enter the vehicle," reported *Aftermarket Business* magazine in 1996. Hence, running boards to provide a manageable intermediate step.

In the typical commuter's car, though, running boards are as extinct as rumble seats. The two hallmarks of the 1930s have entered oblivion together.

all gone

Chapter Three
CLOTHING, GROOMING, AND ORNAMENT

This chapter is risky—of all the things that aren't there anymore, nothing is so likely to come back as fashion. In the months between the writing of this book and its appearance in bookstores, every item mentioned in this section may be back. Even items as seemingly dead as hot pants and poodle skirts may grace the cover of *Vogue*.

The styles that seem likeliest to stay gone are the ones too much associated with a culture that is itself gone. Take love beads. It's hard even to define them—the hippie culture that popularized them wasn't big on precise definitions—but like smut, most people who lived through those years knew them when they saw them. They don't see them much now that hippies are gone.

Then there's the leisure suit, spawn of the 1970s. "Here's a suit you can wear when you're out of the office and into relaxing," said an ad for Knack Leisurewear. "It's a double knit of textured Encron polyester, so it's easy care and easy living in."

"Leisure suits were a middle-class spin-off of hippie clothing, part of the experimentation with menswear and the breakdown of formality," explains Valerie Steele, a fashion historian. But young men, the suits' target market, didn't wear any kind of suits when they didn't have to. The suits themselves, made of all-unnatural fabrics, may exist forever; but leisure suits as a style have "'70s bad taste" written all over them and are gone for good.

Finally, take the opera hat. It derived from the top hat, a widely popular style in the 1800s. Toppers became so tall and narrow—think of Abe Lincoln's stovepipe version—that in the 1820s, the Parisian Antoine Gibus created a popular collapsible version that he managed to patent. The collapsible was first known, naturally, as the Gibus; but after men started wearing it to the opera (one could distinguish it from other toppers in that they were shiny and it was dull), it got the name opera hat, which it has kept ever since. When new entertainments (vaudeville, movies, radio) crowded opera out of mass popularity, they seem to have crowded the opera hat out, too. The hat may not be gone altogether, but it is certainly rare.

Not all extinct styles die because of ties to extinct trends—some get outlawed. In the early part of this century, women wore so many feathers or entire birds on their hats that they were on the verge of wiping out entire species. In the 1920s, Congress made the sale of plumage from American wild birds illegal, and the bird-hat phenomenon declined.

Another fashion that faded was the shirtwaist. It was a woman's blouse tailored like a shirt, with a high, tight collar, long blouson sleeves, and an ornamented bodice. Generally white, this garment remained available for years but became much less fashionable starting in the 1920s, when women went for bolder, more revealing styles.

On the aromatic side of self-adornment, one of the most notorious items was Hai Karate aftershave lotion, popular in the 1970s. In its television commercials, the mild-mannered wearer of this fragrance found his date springing on him in a frenzy of lust so passionate that he had to physically defend himself. The cologne's packaging reportedly included karate instructions for that purpose.

For the ladies, there was Evening in Paris perfume. *The Christian Science Monitor* said of the fragrance, "Well-known in the 1940s, Evening in Paris was once a fixture on the perfume counters of American drug stores. Selling for about $3.00 [the price of a full hair styling with wave or the best seat on Broadway], the fragrance came in trademark cobalt blue bottles…. It evoked images of wartime GIs returning from Paris." Today, American stores don't sell it, although it's available in France as Soir de Paris.

So not all fashions die from trend extinction. Nevertheless, if your look screams "1982 Yuppie" or "1977 punk," it may be time to consider a new wardrobe.

Chest-covering swimsuits for men

In 1935, Atlantic City cops arrested at least 20 men for wearing topless swimsuits. "As recently as 1936," Irving and Amy Wallace and David Wallechinsky write in their book *Significa*, "it was illegal for men to wear topless bathing suits in New York." And, apparently, New Jersey.

A one-piece garment in the early years of the century, with a snug shirt-and-leggings combination coming along later, the long men's bathing suit is an early (and probably unintentional) example of unisex clothes. Straps over the shoulder, V-shaped or scooped neckline, full coverage from mid-chest to thigh (but snug and form-hugging when wet), perfectly horizontal hemline—these styles were characteristic of both men's and women's suits.

The suits were often made of cotton (although wool was popular, too). While attractive and versatile, cotton had problems as swimwear. Anyone who's seen a wet T-shirt contest knows that wet cotton in light colors turns nearly transparent against the body. To keep the body concealed, the suits ran to dark colors like blue and black —but dark colors absorb heat. What's more, wet cotton is heavy to wear. So a man in a dark, wet swimsuit could easily find himself feeling weighted-down, hot, and tired.

The desire for comfort was no doubt a prime motive for the Atlantic City rebellion. It must have been a relief for the men of 1935 to bathe free of their ponderous, clinging shirts, even though (as *Significa* puts it), "The city fathers declared, 'We'll have no gorillas on our beaches.'" The bathers must have been mighty hairy.

But the days of the top-heavy men's swimsuit were dwindling. Topless trunks were less expensive than chest-covering suits, an important factor in cash-starved, Depression-era America. Laws against male toplessness were struck down.

By the end of the '30s, the long swimsuit was virtually gone. Although some of the more unsightly male torsos on today's beaches sometimes make one wish for something dark to cover them, what's done is done.

"Yeah, we're sopping wet. Wanna make something of it?": Swimmers in their suits.

Zoot suits

You can't just stand around, quiet and subdued, in a zoot suit. As subtle as an explosion, this costume is made for strutting and dancing. The jacket droops to mid-thigh or lower, the waist covers the stomach, the shoulders poke into separate time zones, the hat can shade a city block, the watch chain is long enough to rope cattle, and the pants are so baggy that you can fit a child in each leg. The zoot suit even scandalized the government—twice.

No one knows where the suit came from. "[It] has been variously attributed to a Beale Street tailor named Louis Lettes and a Detroit retailer known as Nathan (Toddy) Evans," says the *New York Times*. *Fads: America's Crazes, Fevers and Fancies*, by Peter L. Skolnik, Laura Torbet, and Nikki Smith, says that it had appeared in Harlem by the early 1930s.

Cab Calloway, zoot suitin'.

It wasn't popular among whites until 1941, when Chicago tailor and bandleader Harold Fox glimpsed it on slum teenagers, according to Fox's obituary by Jonathan Eig in the jazz magazine *Down Beat*. Fox outfitted Louis Armstrong, Woody Herman, Stan Kenton, Duke Ellington, Count Basie, Dizzy Gillespie, and other musicians, and his zoot suits traveled as the bands did. "The exaggerated fashion fad blasted away an era of conformity and became a uniform for swinging hipsters of the '40s," Eig says.

Where did the name come from? Fox claims to have invented it. Says Eig, "If something was hip, Fox would say it was 'the end to end all things.' Since the letter Z was the end of the alphabet and his suits were the end of all suits, he coined the name zoot suit."

But the government didn't like the zoot suit. The *Los Angeles Times'* Mary Rourke has written, "Some authority figures had condemned zoot suits as the garb of gangsters and hoodlums. A shortage of wool gave the War Production Board an excuse to ban the style, a glutton for fabric."

Then came the riots. In 1943, Rourke writes, "eleven U.S. sailors said they were provoked by young Mexican Americans they described as zoot suiters. For two weeks after that, several thousand servicemen and civilians wandered the streets, beating up young Latinos, stripping them of their exaggerated jackets and baggy pants." The starch went out of the zoot suit after that.

With the revival of lounge culture and swing dancing, celebrated in the hit independent movie *Swingers*, zoot suits have reappeared, but only occasionally. At least one zoot suit, though, will stay on its wearer forever. Harold Fox died in 1996, age 86, and was buried in a lavender zoot suit.

Nehru jackets

Jawaharlal Nehru (1889–1964) was India's first prime minister, and a prime mover in India's march toward independence. He was also, without knowing it, a fashion leader.

In public, Nehru often wore a single-breasted, hip-length jacket with a banded, standing collar, "adapted from [the] type of coat worn by Indian maharajahs," according to fashion expert Charlotte Mankey Calasibetta in *Fairchild's Dictionary of Fashion*. The coat's slim, straight lines conveyed elegance and self-assurance.

In the middle 1960s, designer Pierre Cardin introduced the Nehru jacket into his Paris shop. The style took off. Rock stars and other young celebrities who needed to look sharp without wearing the square business suit put on Nehrus.

The Monkees in their Nehru jackets.

Clothiers sold Nehru jackets as evening clothes, daywear, and sportswear. The coats came in red velvet, blue silk, and white cotton. (White was, in fact, the coat's traditional color and the one that Nehru himself often wore.) Accessorized with a pendant necklace or love beads instead of a necktie—no tie could fit inside the Nehru's snug collar—it was a coat for the young, chic male of 1967 and '68 to call his own.

Meanwhile, *Vogue* promoted the Nehru jacket to women. It did, after all, resemble chic Chinese dresses, with their simple, straight lines and upright, banded collars.

By the end of the '60s, the Nehru jacket fell out of favor. Exactly why isn't clear, but one theory holds that the fashion establishment had never known exactly what to do with young men who didn't want to wear suits and ties. The Nehru—primarily a man's coat, despite *Vogue*—seemed a way to reach them. But the last thing that most young men wanted was something that the establishment wanted them to wear. They saw Nehru jackets appear on would-be hipsters on TV, and they soon tuned out.

Nehru jackets tried to return. In 1994, the *Christian Science Monitor* reported, "The Nehru jacket is making a comeback...incognito, under the names of 'band collar jacket' and 'the Bombay.'" It didn't exactly sweep the country, although some stores did sell the coats for a while.

Today, the Nehru is an item of nostalgia and even comedy. The movie *Austin Powers: International Man of Mystery*, a 1997 spoof of 1960s spy movies, put the power-mad Dr. Evil (Mike Myers) in a Nehru.

Knickers

Knickers are, essentially, loose short pants tucked in at (or near) the knee. The Dutchmen who settled New York wore them under the name knee breeches; when Washington Irving wrote *A History of New York* (1809) under the somewhat Dutch-sounding name Diedrich Knickerbocker, the pants in the book's illustrations became known as knickerbockers, soon shortened to knickers.

First worn mostly by children, knickers became popular for adults as sportswear. In 1867, the Cincinnati Red Stockings baseball club "replaced the traditional full-length pants with loose-fitting knickers and bright red socks," writes fashion scholar Barbara Schreier in *Men and Women: Dressing the Part*. The style changed the game. "By offering greater freedom of movement than the tight-fitting trousers, knickers accommodated, and even encouraged, more vigorous participation," Schreier says. Soon, other teams took up knickers.

Women wore knickers to participate in the new sport of cycling. "Many leaders of Parisian society had adopted the full knickerbockers and short jacket as their fashionable cycle costume," notes Schreier.

Britain's Prince of Wales (who became Edward VII) wore knickers while hunting. The prince who became Edward VIII and then Duke of Windsor wore them on the golf course. "Knickers were perfect for golfing," journalist John Berendt wrote in *Esquire*. "They enabled a man to forage in the rough without snagging a trouser cuff."

George Bernard Shaw wore knickers, as did Oscar Wilde. They were part of the uniform for some British World War I officers. A postwar vogue for military-type knickers kicked off a wave of popularity that lasted deep into the 1920s.

Knickers started dying in 1929. "The American ambassador to Britain—former vice-president Charles Dawes—flatly refused to wear knee breeches while being presented at court," Berendt wrote. "The last man to win the U.S. Open in a pair of knickers was Gene Sarazin. That was in 1932."

Some athletes still wore them: mountaineers, skiers, and (of course) golfers. In 1989, Berendt wrote, "In recent seasons, pro golfers Payne Stewart and Patty Sheehan have turned up on the golf course in knickers…mail-order catalogs (L.L. Bean and J. Peterman) have begun to offer them, and Ralph Lauren has added them to the Polo line."

While knickers and other short pants have waffled in and out of popularity among women, most men won't go near knickers, on the golf course or anywhere else. As anyone who's been on a beach knows, many men should keep their calves covered.

EYEGLASSES
Pince-nez glasses

Teddy Roosevelt wore them. So did his cousin Franklin, not to mention John Philip Sousa, scientist Louis Pasteur, and innumerable people who weren't famous but liked the idea of eyeglasses that never touched their ears.

No one knows exactly when pince-nez (pronounced pants-nay) glasses were invented, although eyewear historian Richard Corson says in the book *Fashions in Eyeglasses* that they "are believed to have appeared in the 1840s." But no matter where they came from, they soon became popular.

In the 1850s, Corson says, the pince-nez "could be found all over Europe." He adds, "During the latter part of the century, there was a great upsurge in the popularity of the pince-nez for both men and women.… There were heavy rims,

Teddy Roosevelt and his pince-nez.

light rims, and no rims at all; there were ribbons, chains, and unanchored glasses which the wearer hoped would not fall off and smash; there were round lenses, oval lenses, half-moon lenses, and rectangular lenses; and above all, there was a wide variety of nosepieces for holding the glasses on."

The pince-nez remained popular into the 20th century. Young men wore them at fashionable parties. By 1913, a newspaper society report called a pince-nez "the correct style for evening wear...hung to a black moire or plain silk braid...one-quarter to five-sixteenths of an inch wide." In 1921, the pamphlet *Be Beautiful in Glasses* advised, "For full dress, gold-mounted rimless pince-nez are refinement itself and absolutely correct."

Having passed from a sign of smart fashion to one of good taste, the pince-nez had nowhere to go but dull conventionality. In 1930, humorist P.G. Wodehouse said in advice to novelists that the pince-nez "may be worn by good college professors, bank presidents, and [classical] musicians. No bad man may wear pince-nez."

When pince-nez wearer Franklin Roosevelt died in 1945, the pince-nez died with him. Occasionally, it would pop up in movies on the nose of a crabby oldster who'd whip it off to shake it in the face of the hero while crackling, "Now, see here, young man. We'll have no more of your foolishness! Why, in my day..."

But otherwise, the pince-nez was gone.

NOT QUITE GONE, BUT MIGHTY SCARCE
Lorgnettes

Lorgnettes are the snob's spectacles, perfect for snooty glances down one's nose at the unfashionable. There's something so pretentious about eyeglasses with handles.

Lorgnettes go back quite a ways. "[A] forerunner of the lorgnette appeared in an illustration on the wall of the monastery of St. Marco of Florence in the 14th century," says J. William Rosenthal, M.D., author of *Spectacles and Other Vision Aids: A History and Guide to Collecting*. By the 18th century, aristocratic Japanese were using them. But the lorgnette truly flourished in Europe.

Its name comes from the French word *lorgner*, meaning to stare or leer. Originally, lorgnette was the name of a tiny telescope that the gentry used at the opera and other events. It's not clear how the English took the word into their language as the name of another kind of eyewear.

In 1780, English optician George Adams developed the first true lorgnette; 45 years later, his colleague Robert Betell Bate patented lorgnettes with handles (previously, they'd had round finger clips, like rings). Even then, says Rosenthal, "public use of the lorgnette was decried as poor decorum because it was often used for ogling neighbors or strangers."

Gradually, lorgnettes came into fashion. There were folding lorgnettes, spring-loaded lorgnettes, monocle lorgnettes, even double lorgnettes for people who needed different lenses for distance and reading. Lorgnettes were attached to fans, ear trumpets, lockets, lapel clips, gold chains, and tiny mirrors. Their frames and handles were made of gold or silver, encrusted with diamonds, sapphires, or jade, carved in elaborate designs or decorated with miniature paintings. For the less affluent, there were plain lorgnettes made of unornamented tortoiseshell.

Early in the 20th century, lorgnettes suffered criticism as pointless affectations ("little more than playthings," said one optician). They were no longer a faddish rage. But they stuck around and were still visible on the noses of the rich and fashionable.

They even reached out to the non-wealthy classes. In the 1950s, women's fashion magazines touted lorgnettes "for reading menus or looking up telephone numbers." In the '60s, opticians stocked lorgnettes with plastic frames.

Even today, one can still find lorgnettes on a few faces, but there's no ignoring the truth: Lorgnettes have been on the wane for decades. The only eyewear that requires hand-holding, the snotty yet cute little lorgnette is today a rarity.

HEADGEAR
Bonnets

If any article of fashion should have stuck around forever, it's the woman's bonnet. Attractive, practical, and versatile, it flourished for centuries.

"The word 'bonnet' once meant a man's hat, not a woman's," wrote journalist Bill Severn in his book *Here's Your Hat*. "There was a coarse green woolen cloth known as 'bonet' that was popular for men's hats in the Middle Ages, and the term

Nothing like a bonnet to give the old gal a thrill.

'bonnet' came into use to describe any masculine hat or cap.... Some costume experts argue that the head covering shown in most pictures of England's legendary hero-outlaw, Robin Hood, really was a bonnet and not a hood."

"It wasn't until the end of the 18th century that the name was given to feminine headwear," Severn adds. Bonnets were defined as a brimless or thin-brimmed hat that fit over the top and back of the head, secured by a ribbon below the chin.

Bonnets, popular in England, eventually came to America. Women of all classes wore them. "Popular bonnets of the 1800s were made of nearly every available material, ranging from velvet, silk, felt, kid, and taffeta to horsehair, straw, organdy, and lace," Severn reports.

The Victorian era (1837–1901) was the bonnet's glory. "During the early Victorian period, [the bonnet] was not merely popular but was considered to be the only correct form of outdoor head covering except for the most informal occasions," says fashion expert Georgine de Courtais in her *Women's Headdress and Hairstyles*. She adds that bonnets got very elaborate: "The trimmings of bonnets during this period consisted of ribbons, feathers, and flowers." Later, bonnets sported fruit, wings, and whole birds.

In sunny climates, bonnets were plain, working hats. "The sunbonnet—which came to symbolize female pioneers—was a practical and inexpensive way of protecting the head and shading the eyes," writes historian Lee Hall in *Common Threads: A Parade of American Clothing*.

After most Americans moved from the frontier to the city, they wanted slicker, more modern wear. Older women wore bonnets, as did Salvation Army ladies and some nurses, but not fashion trendsetters. By the time Irving Berlin wrote "Easter Parade" ("In your Easter bonnet with all the frills upon it, you'll be the grandest lady in the Easter parade"), most women wore bonnets only to recapture the high fashion of an earlier age.

But if global warming makes the whole planet as sunny as the Southwestern prairie, the May 2018 *Vogue* may trumpet, "The Return of the Bonnet!"

Coonskin caps

Born on a mountain top in Tennessee,
Kilt him a b'ar when he was only three.
An' just 'fore his fad could go collapse,
Sold him a boatload o' coonskin caps.
Day-vee...Davy Crockett!
King o' the wild headgear!

Davy played by Fess Parker.

The song didn't go quite like that (apologies to composers Tom Blackburn and George Bruns), but it may as well have. The round raccoon-fur hat, complete with tail, was a nationwide sensation. In their book *The Disney Studio Story*, authors Richard Hollis and Brian Sibley note that at least 10 million coonskin caps were sold during the craze.

It began in December 1954, when the Disneyland anthology TV series "had an enormous, and quite unexpected, success with three films on the life of Davy Crockett," say Hollis and Sibley. Kids begged their parents for Crockett rifles, clothes, guitars, tents, pocketknives, lunch boxes, and, of course, caps. Ironically (according to *The Whole Pop Catalog*, by the Berkeley Pop Culture Project), Fess Parker, who played Crockett, hated the caps.

He may have been the only one. The Readers' Digest Association's compendium *Our Glorious Century* says, "At the height of the Davy Crockett hysteria in 1955, the opportunity to get a real coonskin cap caused near riots by youthful Crockett fanatics." Even democratic presidential candidate Estes Kefauver campaigned wearing one of the hats and got vast publicity.

He picked the wrong hat. As *Our Glorious Century* points out, "Davy the man had lived for 50 years; Davy the fad barely made it to 11 months." In 1957, clothing manufacturers were making raccoon coats from leftover cap materials. Kefauver lost the presidential nomination to Adlai Stevenson. Millions of caps sat in closets or trash cans, forgotten.

You might be able to find a coonskin cap in a vintage-clothing store. Still, wearing such a cap today can't provide the same thrill as sitting in front of your family's television set, wearing your own coonskin cap, and singing along with the TV about the King of the Wild Frontier.

The height of style.

Cloche hats

The flapper. You can always spot one of the bright young things of the 1920s by her fringed and very short skirt, pale features, slim frame—and atop them all, hugging her head, the simple but striking straw or felt cloche hat. With a name derived appropriately from the French word for bell, and a shape sometimes like a bell but often described as a helmet, the cloche symbolized the young, emancipated female.

England's Queen Charlotte wore the first cloche—a big, muslin number—in the late 1770s. The Charlotte (as it was named) was popular in both England and France for decades.

The small cloche came to life in the 1920s. While fashionable hats of earlier years were ornate creations with fancy feathers and pins, the new, nearly brimless cloche was as streamlined and modern as the 20th Century Limited. And unlike fancier hats, with their fragile clouds of gauzy fabric, the cloche (which covered the hair, the ears, and often the forehead and the back of the neck) was practical: "This head-hugging hat was as storm-proof as a flying helmet," says Jacqueline Herald, author of *Fashions of a Decade: The 1920s.*

Yet it wasn't dull. There were cloches for day and evening, winter and summer, even for skiing. They came in various colors, with trimming of leather or fur. While the prominent Paris designer Reboux offered a cloche with no decoration at all, some cloche wearers slipped on a buckle, jewel, feather, pin, or brooch.

The most common decoration was a ribbon. Says Herald, "The tying of the ribbon carried a coded message: arrow-like, it indicated the single girl who had already given her promise of love; the firm knot meant she was married; but a flirtatious bow was the symbol of the independent, fancy-free girl."

Cloches stayed popular through the 1920s, but a new decade brought new styles. Movie stars like Greta Garbo and Joan Crawford popularized shoulder-length hair, a style too voluminous to fit inside a cloche. Cloches went away.

They came back after the Depression and World War II—although as designer David Bond observed in *The Guinness Guide to 20th Century Fashion*, "the newer styles were softer and showed more of the face and the hair."

They didn't last long. The cloche made another stand in the 1960s—for instance, a version graced Ali MacGraw in the hit movie *Love Story* (1970)—but it was as brief one. Unlike the T-shirt or little black dress, the cloche was cute but not classic; it wasn't a perennial fashion but only a passing fad.

FOOTWEAR
Spats

When a filmmaker or a cartoonist wants to show an aging man as old-fashioned and self-important, he often covers the man's shoes in spats.

Spat is short for spatterdash, which the dictionary defines as "a long legging formerly worn to protect the stocking or trouser leg, as in wet weather"—in other words, to repel spatters from rain or puddles.

Spats were born of the 17th-century fashion for tall boots. As author June Swann writes in her book *Shoes*, "the amount of leather in the [tall] boot inevitably meant a very expensive boot." Non-leather boots were cheaper but more vulnerable to damage. To protect them, men wore spats, "most being of leather, with some suede, and fastening up the side with interlocking loops drawn through 'buttonholes,'" Swann writes.

Jimmy Stewart, uncomfortable in spats, in *Mr. Smith Goes to Washington*.

After the tall boot fell from fashion, spats stayed on, though they changed. "In 1802," reports Florence Ledger in *Put Your Foot Down: A Treatise on the History of Shoes*, "'spats,' the shortened version of the spatterdash, reached only a little above the ankle." These spats, writes historian Everett Wilson in *Vanishing Americana*, "were worn on formal occasions with...patent leather dancing pumps and also when walking in the snow with low shoes." By then worn more for fashion than protection, spats were made of felt or wool, usually in beige, gray, or white.

Spats hit a peak in the early 1900s. Many roads weren't paved for autos, which left ruts that became mud puddles when rain fell. According to Boston haberdasher Len Goldstein, rich men wore spats "to protect their spiffy shoes...from the mud."

Possibly because spats protected shoes so well, men in uniform adopted them. "During World War I, doughboys wore a version of them, called 'leggings,'" the *Christian Science Monitor*'s Yvonne Zipp notes. "Boy Scouts donned canvas versions as part of their uniforms until 1919."

After the war, spats went to the movies. "Al Jolson sported a pair of spats in *The Jazz Singer*," says Zipp. W.C. Fields wore them, too.

"Spats were widely used until World War II, after which paved roads made them obsolete," Zipp says. "There just wasn't as much mud to spatter." They weren't completely dead—"today, you can sometimes spot them on the legs of marching bands," Zipp observes—but they were definitely relics of the past.

So long, spats. From rich man's affectation to doughboy's pal, you served well. And you still do, helping the cartoonist or filmmaker portray an old-fashioned man who wants the world to think he's important.

Garters for men

Garters go back surprisingly far. Around 4000 B.C., men were wearing knee garters as ornaments. But the style truly came into its own in the 14th century A.D. European portraits from the time clearly show men wearing the little bands, sometimes on only one leg—a sure sign that garters were not practical but strictly ornamental.

By the early 1500s, male style meant gams. Slim, shapely legs were crucial to manly good looks. Men wore kilt-like short robes and drew eyes to their legs by wearing silk garters tied in fancy bows.

Even after the fashion for male leg shows wore off, garters stuck around, and finally found a way to be useful. When men switched from hose to stockings that ended below the knee, they found a problem: their socks, made of cotton and wool, weren't elastic enough to grip their calves. The socks tended to fall, settling around the ankle in a sloppy clump.

Hence the elastic garter, which now attached to the sock not by knots or bows but by simple clips, buttons, or clasps. "The Flexo," an ad from 1896 announced, "fits the calf of the leg smoothly without binding, lays flat, has rubber shank to prevent tearing the hose. Its metal parts conform to the shape of the leg. The silk finish webbing is handsome—durable. You don't feel 'harnessed up.'" Not a bad deal for 25 cents a pair.

The 1950s brought doom to the garter. A burst of new synthetic fibers (nylon, Orlon, Rayon, Lycra, and others) included elastics. Sock makers sewed the fabrics into the tops of socks, and they gripped calves nicely. No more need a man concern himself with falling socks. No more did a man need to buy garters.

Garters are still around, but not usually on men's legs. In saloons with "gay '90s" decor, the bartenders sometimes wear garters on their sleeves—for adornment, not to keep the sleeves from slipping off. At weddings, many a bride throws her strictly ornamental leg garter at the unmarried men, just as she tosses her bouquet at the single women. And the kinkier among us delight in gartered ladies' hose.

But only the most fetishistic souls have sweaty fantasies about male garters. The little band that adorned the men of the Bronze Age and was fit for a king in the days of Rabelais is now a bit of history.

Earth Shoes

"More devastating than a fire storm…deadlier than a neutron bomb…more widely spread than MX missile sites. This was the tragedy of the mid-1970s—the Earth Shoe." So wrote humorist Mimi Pond in the mid-1980s.

What was she talking about, and what made the Earth Shoe a menace to fashionable feet everywhere?

It wasn't just that Earth Shoes were bland, although they were: thick, ridged soles supporting a boxy, smooth-surfaced top, without fancy stitching, punch holes, or other decoration. What made them famous was their "negative heel." It made the wearer's toes ride higher than her heels.

Designed in 1957 by Copenhagen yoga instructor Anne Kalsø, the Earth Shoe's sole allegedly duplicated the impression of a foot walking barefoot in sand. This design was to give the shoe a more "natural" shape and give the body better posture.

Rising public awareness of ecology brought the Earth Shoe to prominence, wrote *Time* magazine's Linda Lofaro. "The shoes were first marketed in the U.S. under license by Raymond and Eleanor Jacobs in 1970. Impressed by Earth Day crowds gathering near their just-opened store in New York City, the Jacobses made a snap

This fella seems pretty happy to be standing without his pants; it must be the garters.

decision to change the name of their product that very day from Anne Kalsø Minus Heel Shoes to Earth Shoes."

A back-to-nature trend was swinging along (the Roots brand of similarly "natural" shoes was selling well), and the Jacobses benefited. "The couple soon found themselves presiding over a multimillion-dollar business," Lofaro wrote. "At the height of their popularity, Earth Shoes were available in dozens of styles: sandals, clogs, hiking shoes, and deluxe, fleece-lined ankle boots." Actors Tony Curtis and James Coburn, and Olympic athlete Mark Spitz, wore Earth Shoes. In 1976, according to *The Encyclopedia of Pop Culture* by Jane and Michael Stern, "there were 135 Earth Shoe stores around the country."

But many "back-to-nature" enthusiasts found that they didn't like Earth Shoes. Feet accustomed to shoe heels that rose higher than the toes found the shoes uncomfortable. After peaking in the mid-'70s, Earth Shoe sales fell. "In 1977, after a dispute with banks, the company was placed in bankruptcy," says Lofaro.

"Today, bring up the subject of the Earth Shoe at a party, and people laugh nervously and change the subject quickly. They deny ever having worn them or defensively admit that they were only following fashion," writes Pond. "We are a nation shamed."

Like other fashion trends, Earth Shoes occasionally threaten a comeback. Fortunately, Pond has a recipe for preventing it. "The answer is not to be led down the garden path of fashion folly.... Remember, when all shoes are stupid, only the stupid will wear shoes."

WRISTWATCHES
Watches that need winding

It was a morning ritual: wake up, grab your watch, and wind it. Tiny grooves bit into your thumb and index finger as you turned the round stem at the edge of the watch's face. You felt increasing resistance as you wound, until the watch wouldn't let you wind any more.

You had to wind the watch because it was driven by an internal spring. As the spring loosened, it drove the watch's hands; but it needed to be tightened every day. If left untightened, it ran down and showed the wrong time.

Watchmakers started fitting tiny clocks into bracelets in the late 1500s or early

1600s. They all needed winding. Around 1770, watchmaker Abraham Louis Perrelet built an automatic, self-winding pocket watch—but, notes *Wristwatches: History of a Century's Development* by Helmut Kahlert, Richard Muhe, and Gisbert Brunner, "automatic winding remained…more a technical joke or a refined accessory than a general procedure."

In 1924, Englishman John Harwood patented a self-winding wristwatch. It failed commercially—"too-high price, management errors, and above all the effects of the world economic crisis [the Depression], say some, while others note technical production difficulties and conceptual weaknesses," says *Wristwatches*.

Turn the stem and wind it up: yesterday's watch.

But then came quartz. Around 1900, "[scientist] Pierre Curie observed [that]…certain crystals, among them quartz crystals, actually vibrate mechanically—change shape back and forth—when an alternating current of electricity passes through them," historian David Landes writes in *Revolution in Time: Clocks and the Making of the Modern World*. "[The] crystals could be made to produce stable vibrations—that is, could serve as a clock."

The first quartz clocks were built in the 1920s. But, says Landes, decades passed "before quartz clocks were miniaturized enough to be suitable for personal wear."

They weren't instantly popular. "The earliest models (1968–69) cost upward of a thousand dollars," Landes says. "They were bulky…. The user had to press a button to read the time, not an easy thing to do when one is carrying a case in one hand and hurrying to catch a train…. [And] these early models were not so reliable as conventional mechanical timepieces."

Watch companies fixed these problems and added features that winding watches didn't have, such as calculators, stopwatches, and calendars. They effectively killed the winding watch.

Landes says, "The quartz watch is surely not the last word." The future will offer newer and better wristwatches.

But none of them will need winding.

It's always time for Spiro!

Spiro Agnew watches

Vice presidents are usually unobtrusive, but not Spiro Agnew. Richard Nixon's White House deployed him to attack liberals, the press, and anyone else it opposed.

College students made fun of Agnew. A campus joke of the time: "Have you heard that Mickey Mouse is wearing a Spiro Agnew watch?"

Not a great joke. But at Christmas 1969, student Stephen Dougherty told it to his father, Dr. Hale Dougherty of Anaheim, California. The joke inspired the older man. Why not make a Spiro Agnew watch?

For the watch's face, Dr. Dougherty hired art student Bill Buerge to draw a cartoon of Agnew. Buerge put him in a stars-and-stripes outfit, fingers in the V-shaped "peace sign," arms as the minute and hour hands. Dougherty formed a company called Dirty Time, hired a Swiss firm to make 2,000 watches, and priced them at $14.95 apiece.

They sold out in a week. Over the next two months, another 5,000 sold. Major stores ordered 50,000 more. Ethel Kennedy wore one; her brother-in-law, liberal senator Ted Kennedy, asked her what the watch did. "She told me, 'You wind it up, and it criticizes your brother-in-law!'"

Dirty Time sent a watch to Agnew himself. He called the watch "attractive and clever," and gave it to his daughter Kim. He also said, via his attorney, that he hadn't allowed the use of his likeness but would if Dirty Time "would turn over a substantial portion of any profit to families of Americans captured or missing in Southeast Asia."

Dougherty refused. To comply, he said, "would be a recognition of the right of politicians to control and therefore stifle political comment."

Other firms didn't mind. American Time Company and Varsity House, Inc. made Agnew watches and in July donated $10,000 apiece, which went to the National League of Families of American Prisoners Missing in Southeast Asia as well as the American Indian Self Help Program of Save the Children Foundation. A month later, Precision Watch Company donated $10,000, which Agnew turned over to the Salesian Boys Club of Los Angeles, a group helping Hispanic kids. Meanwhile, Dirty Time sued another firm, Hudson Watch Company, as well as S. Klein Department Stores for copying his watch and infringing on its copyright.

The watch's popularity seemed to inspire other industries. In 1971, toymakers announced plans for "a Spiro Agnew board game, a Spiro Agnew jigsaw puzzle, and a miniature drag racer bearing his likeness," wrote reporter Leonard Sloane in the *New York Times*.

Soon, the vogue for Spiro watches faded. The vice president resigned in 1973 after being accused of taking bribes and died in 1996.

HAIRSTYLES
Not quite gone, but mighty scarce
Beehive hairstyle

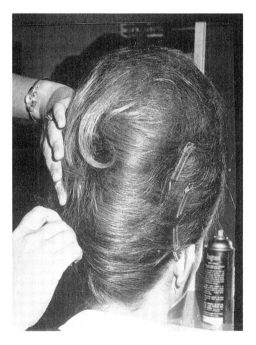

The late 1950s and early '60s were the time of BIG. Cadillac tailfins were big. Jayne Mansfield's breasts were big. Movies were big (see the section on Cinerama). Bigger was better, and there was no hairstyle bigger than the beehive.

The beehive looked like one—a rounded, honeycomb-shaped hair cone. Upswept and practically rock solid, each strand virtually waxed into place, a beehive towered high, swoops of follicles piled on each other or swirling skyward.

Some beehives were as big as the owner's entire head. Some were bigger. Some beehive wearers had to stoop to pass through doorways.

It was the perfect hairstyle for the teenager or working gal who wanted to look grown-up and glamorous, and make sure that everyone knew it. Girl groups, such as the Marvelettes, Shirelles, and Ronettes—often not long out of high school or a no-future factory/pink-collar job—wore beehives. So did Aretha Franklin.

How do you style—or, more accurately, construct—a perfect beehive? *The Whole Pop Catalog*, by the Berkeley Pop Culture Project, describes one

Too much style: the beehive at its best.

45

method. "You need teasing, extra hairpieces, structural frames of wire or plastic, and lots and lots of hair spray—the cheaper the better, hole in the ozone layer be damned. Legend has it that the biggest, stiffest beehives were those least washed, with the most lacquer build-up. Then there were those urban legends about colonies of insects living inside them."

The beehive faded as the more natural look of the middle '60s took over. From Janis Joplin to Gloria Steinem, women let their hair cascade loosely about their shoulders. Others, such as Julie Andrews, Goldie Hawn, and Twiggy, kept theirs boyishly short. African-American women such as Angela Davis and Pam Grier wore afros and other "natural" styles.

The beehive was no longer merely out of fashion, ready like other fashions to await its return to favor. It was obsolete, ludicrous, cornball.

Yet it lives on. The women in the pop group The B-52s (named after a particularly aggressive beehive style) have worn them. Cult filmmaker John Waters celebrated them in his movie *Hairspray*. A Broadway musical about the early '60s girl groups was called *Beehive*. The 'hive was still corny, but it was being celebrated for its corn.

The beehive was a hairstyle with guts—it demanded attention. It may be gone, but will ever stand tall in our memories, in our hearts, and in whatever part of our brain makes us giggle uncontrollably at the sight of silliness.

all gone

Chapter Four
ENTERTAINMENT

Why does a form of entertainment that enthralls a good portion of the planet simply die?

If you look at long-gone movie trends, it's hard to find a pattern. Silent movies, with the accompaniment of a pianist or even a full-pit orchestra and renowned stars such as Mary Pickford and Douglas Fairbanks, lost their glimmer when sound took over in the late 1920s. Travelogues left the theaters when all short films, from cartoons to newsreels, began fading in the '50s. Smell-o-Vision offered aromas to match the action on screen, but the public didn't care. And ratings have simply changed: The M rating for mature-audience movies has been replaced by R and NC-17.

The test pattern's on. Go to bed!

Television, of course, used to produce and discard endless series. These days, though, the past is back. Go to your video store, and *I Love Lucy* is there, as are old *Saturday Night Live* episodes. The Sci-Fi Channel, Nick at Nite's TV Land, the Cartoon Network—they're filled with old shows. Yesterday's nightly news clips get play on today's news to illustrate a point about how public life has changed (or hasn't changed). Museums throw tributes to *The Dick Van Dyke Show* or *M*A*S*H*. And of course, *Star Trek* never goes away.

Still, some pieces of television don't return. Talkfests such as *The Mike Douglas Show* seem lost in the ether, and when tabloid TV series such as *A Current Affair* go off the air, they usually go for good. In late night, infomercials have replaced test patterns and preachers have stopped doing sermonettes, instead becoming flamboyant televangelists with their own cable-TV empires.

Music, meanwhile, bends to the breezes of technology, abandoning old machines when new ones come along. High-fidelity stereo speakers replaced the old, flaring gramophone horn. The reel-to-reel tape recorder replaced the wire machine, and millions of people first heard their own recorded voices on them, until eight-track tapes, cassettes, and then compact discs took over.

It isn't always machinery that kills a musical trend. Many an immigrant (especially from Italy) who needed a way to make a living picked up a hand-cranked barrel organ and a cute monkey, and became a street entertainer. Technology may not have shoved them off the streets, but off they went anyway.

Some now-defunct forms died when other entertainments outpaced them. Americans abandoned Beta home video systems for VHS because they could get a wider variety of more popular movies on VHS. They loved Pong, an early video ping-pong game, but ignored it when flashier games came along. Radio soap operas commanded the attention of millions until television started pulling the millions away, at which point the radio shows quit their home medium and moved to TV.

Why does a form of entertainment that enthralls a good portion of the planet simply die? Pick a reason, any reason. You'll probably be right.

MOVIES
Motion Picture Production Code

It wasn't meant for censorship. It was meant to keep rich, young hedonists from having dangerous fun.

1922. Comedian Fatty Arbuckle is arrested for raping a woman to death. Stars Mary Miles Minter and Mabel Normand are implicated in the murder of director William Desmond Taylor. Wallace Reid, who plays clean-cut heroes, dies of heroin addiction. Meanwhile, the movies celebrate seduction (Rudolph Valentino), decadence (Erich von Stroheim), and hunger for luxury (Gloria Swanson).

Defenders of morality condemned Hollywood. "The protests rapidly assumed the form of a threatened national censorship of all movies," writes film critic Arthur Knight in *The Liveliest Art: A Panoramic History of the Movies*.

To stop the wave, film executives formed the Motion Picture Producers and

Distributors of America and to run it hired Will Hays—"a Presbyterian elder, chairman of the Republican National Committee, and at the time Postmaster General," says Knight. Hays' office forbade "licentious or suggestive nudity," "ridicule of clergy," and "inference of sexual perversion," among other things— but as film historian Ethan Mordden puts it in *Movie Star: A Look at the Women Who Made Hollywood*, "Hays' main job was policing the town, checking up on what movie personnel did on the personal rather than professional level."

By the early '30s, Hays didn't need to control the stars much—the studios had started doing it—but the movies themselves were stretching the code's limits. Decency groups threatened boycotts over violent gangster films and Mae West's sexual innuendoes.

The Hays office bore down: no on-screen seduction, nudity (even for babies), sleeping together (even for spouses), or brutality. Hays' office fought producer David Selznick over *Gone with the Wind*'s "Frankly, my dear, I don't give a damn," forced a bordello scene out of *Citizen Kane,* and even made Walt Disney put flower necklaces on nude centaurettes in *Fantasia*.

A newsreel camera-man at the ready.

In 1953, the Hays office ordered director Otto Preminger to cut the words *virgin*, *seduce*, and *pregnant* from *The Moon Is Blue*. He refused. The resulting scandal helped make the movie a hit. In 1966, the office objected to the raw language of Warner Bros.' *Who's Afraid of Virginia Woolf?* "Studio boss Jack L. Warner refused to soften on the subject, and the film eventually received an 'R' rating...becoming the first film under the new rating system to carry this designation," writes Susan Sackett in *The Hollywood Reporter Book of Box Office Hits*.

The ratings replaced the code. Movies soon could say or show almost anything.

Newsreels

When you went to the movies, you got the news. It came before the main feature in a short anthology of clips: the president giving a speech, an earthquake overseas, troops in battle, factory workers on strike, a scientist showing a new invention, an athlete pushing himself to victory, the almost human antics of a cute animal, and something involving a pretty girl. One observer called them "jumpy little post-card collections"; another, humorist Oscar Levant, dubbed the typical newsreel "a series of catastrophes followed by a fashion show."

Newsreels are almost as old as movie exhibition. As early as 1910, the French film company Pathe was producing one-reel news shorts. Its American arm started exhibiting them in 1911.

Others followed. "At its height, in the United States alone, the American newsreel was seen weekly by at least 40 million people, and throughout the world by more than 200 million," says film historian Raymond Fielding, author of *The American Newsreel, 1911–1967*. "For many people, especially the illiterate, it was a principal source of news."

Some of the newsreels' most striking images came during World War II: Japan's attack on Pearl Harbor, Hitler's dance when the Nazis conquered France (a doctored, even phony clip), and the desperate battles of D-Day.

Mostly, though, newsreels weren't good journalism. "Newsreels were compromised from the beginning by fakery, re-creation, and staging," says Fielding. "Because of [the newsreel's] brief 9–10-minute length and its coverage of so many different subjects, the treatment of any one event was sketchy and inadequate."

Newsreels started dying in the late 1940s. Most of the studios that made newsreels owned movie theaters; but in 1948, the Justice Department forced the studios to dump the theaters. Cut off from a key source of revenue, studios chopped costs. "The newsreels had never made any money for anyone, and so they were the first to go," says Fielding.

Besides, television news was coming along, providing faster coverage. "By the time our print got to the theater, it was much too late," said a Hearst "News of the Day" spokesman. And as *Newsweek* pointed out, "Feature films have increasingly filled up or even stretched the movie theater's time budget, leaving little need for fillers."

Time magazine killed its newsreel operations in 1951, Warner Bros. in '56, Paramount in '57, Fox in '63, and, finally, Hearst and Universal—the last majors—in '67. Today, the closest that most people get to newsreels is occasional clips on television or *Citizen Kane*'s brassy parody, "News on the March." Fittingly, that pastiche of a dead form is devoted to an obituary.

Super 8 home movies

Yanking the portable screen's tripod legs into place, pulling the screen from its steel-gray housing, threading film through a projector's intricate gearworks; the flutter and clatter as the film rips through the projector, the screaming-white gush of light from the lens—this was the experience of home movies. The moviemaker gathers family and friends on the couch and floor of the living room and narrates the film's silent action (while the audience interrupts with questions and jokes): relatives waving in front of the new house; Mom and Dad at Yosemite Falls; the oldest son's experimental, frame-by-frame animation of paper cut-outs.

It began on August 12, 1923, when the Victor Animatograph Company of Davenport, Iowa, began advertising the first portable movie camera. "It was three by six by eight inches, weighed five pounds, and cost $55," reports *Famous First Facts*, by Joseph Nathan Kane, Steven Anzovin, and Janet Podell. Around the same time, Kodak offered a developing and processing service.

The camera and its projector.

Still, home filming wasn't a ubiquitous constant until the 1960s. The birth of the easy-to-use Super 8 camera (named after its film, eight millimeters wide) coincided with the prosperous economy and the baby boom's millions of cute, active kids to make the purchase of a home movie camera a natural.

By 1978, "one in every three houses had a Super 8," says Philip Vigeant, owner of the camera store Super 8 Sound. "That year, Kodak sold 100 million rolls of Super 8 film." Thirty million households made homegrown flicks.

Then came video. The home camcorder's cartridges captured more action than Super 8's three-minute spools. Showing videos didn't require setting up a screen or threading a projector. And they had sound.

Super 8 didn't go away entirely. Many film schools ordered students to shoot their first films in Super 8. "In the late '80s, advertisers like Nike, Honda, Canada Dry, and McDonald's made Super 8s grainy look fashionable," wrote American Film's Randall Tierney. "Rock videos—like Paula Abdul's black-and-white 'Straight Up' and Guns N' Roses' 'Sweet Child O' Mine'—now appreciate its grittiness." Even some theatrical movies, such as *Black Rain*, *Flatliners*, and the Neil Young documentary *The Year of the Horse*, have featured Super 8.

Super 8 is no longer a part of every family occasion, but it's a great document of ordinary life. In a report on home-movie screenings at London's Museum of the

Moving Image, the *London Times'* Sean Coughlan wrote, "This rather accidental form of history projects a real sense of time and place, with the pictures tinged with a rather ghostly poignancy.... Any [college's] history department would do well to have such vivid illustrations."

Cinerama

Big. Very big. Unbelievably big. That was Cinerama.

Before Cinerama, movies were made in an aspect ratio of 1.33 to 1—that is, the image on screen was a third wider than it was tall. It's the shape of most television screens.

Film revenues fell in the late 1940s and early '50s, and movie executives blamed TV. Special effects expert Fred Waller found a solution: a movie camera with three lenses. When a film shot in this system, dubbed Cinerama, was projected on three side-by-side curving screens, its aspect ratio was a boggling 2.65 to 1, nearly twice as wide as conventional movies. At 97 feet wide and about 37 feet high, Cinerama offered an image more than 2,500 times the size of a 21-inch TV screen.

The first Cinerama feature, naturally called *This Is Cinerama*, was released in 1952. The movie, a travelogue, took audiences over a roller coaster, on a gondola ride in Venice, to a bullfight in Spain, and, finally, into "a stirring flyover of the United States...set to the music of the Mormon Tabernacle Choir," according to *The Hollywood Reporter Book of Box Office Hits* by Susan Sackett. The movie grossed more than $15 million. (The previous year's biggest hit, *Quo Vadis?*, earned less than $12 million.)

Metro-Goldwyn-Mayer, the first major studio to make Cinerama films, released *The Wonderful World of the Brothers Grimm* and *How the West Was Won* in 1962. "When the opening shot faded in—a huge aerial vista—I instinctively grabbed my arm rests," *Film Comment* magazine's David Joachim says about *West*. "I was no longer watching a movie that happened to begin with an aerial shot of mountains—I was flying over those mountains.... By the finale, I was a physical and emotional wreck."

West and *Grimm* became hits. So did Cinerama. "At its peak in the early 1960s," the *Hollywood Reporter* has said, "Cinerama was shown in 240 theaters around the world."

Then came the fall. "It was five to six times more expensive to shoot Cinerama scenes [than conventional scenes]," the *Reporter* says. "Theater owners eventually abandoned the curved screens in favor of today's flat, rubber-coated canvas ones because they could get more seats in the theater [with flat screens]."

By 1997, New Neon Movies in Dayton, Ohio, was America's only Cinerama theater. In September, slow ticket sales forced the New Neon to stop showing Cinerama. "Only the National Museum of Photography, Film and Television in Bradford, England, will still show the films," the *Reporter* announced. (Although some theaters, such as Hollywood's Cinerama Dome, call themselves Cinerama, they don't feature the authentic process.)

Cinerama's legacy holds on. Other processes followed. Today, the standard aspect ratio for theatrical films is 1.85 to 1—not as wide as Cinerama, but wider than the earlier 1.33 to 1. With high-definition television using an ratio of 1.78 to 1, Cinerama's wide-screen revolution will remain with us for years.

Buy a DuMont, fund an entire network.

TELEVISION
DuMont Television Network

The original fourth network, DuMont was. It had "more firsts than Adam," wrote journalist Jeff Kisseloff in *The Box: An Oral History of Television, 1920–1961*. "It produced the first live network broadcast…the first regularly scheduled children's show…the first daytime schedule. It was the first to regularly broadcast pro football. It was on DuMont's *Cavalcade of Stars* that Ralph Kramden first threatened to send Alice to the moon."

It began with engineer Allen DuMont, who, in 1931, created a TV picture tube that could last 10 times longer than any others, including those by powerhouse RCA. Soon thereafter, he set up manufacturing.

In 1938, DuMont decided to start broadcasting. "He borrowed $200,000 to start a flagship station in Manhattan," reports Michael Ritchie in his book *Please Stand By: A Prehistory of Television*.

By 1944, DuMont was broadcasting four nights a week. He bought a station in Washington, creating a "network" of sorts. In 1946, DuMont aired what is arguably the very first network show, featuring the mayor of New York, a game show, and a one-act play.

ONLY **DU MONT** WILL DO

ctor Series **DU MONT**
"first with the finest in television"

DuMont's network added more than 175 affiliates. It aired the New York Yankees, the National Football League, and network TV's first World Series. It had Jackie Gleason, Bishop Fulton Sheen (whose audiences were nearly as big as top-rated comedian Milton Berle), comedy innovator Ernie Kovacs, and a popular amateur hour.

But broadcasting is costly. "While CBS and NBC could rely on radio income to subsidize their TV networks, DuMont's only other income came from the sale of its TV sets, which was not enough to make up the deficit," says Ritchie. Even small, young ABC got $30 million from the movie-house chain United Paramount Theaters. By 1951, DuMont was more than a million dollars in debt.

DuMont had another problem. Local TV stations made good money. Other networks owned five stations apiece, the maximum that the Federal Communications Commission allowed. DuMont, with three stations, naturally wanted more. But one of its backers, Paramount Pictures, had two stations of its own. DuMont didn't control the stations (at least one wasn't even a DuMont affiliate), but the FCC counted them as DuMont stations and refused to let the network buy more, keeping it behind the competition.

By mid-1955, DuMont had lost $16 million. The men in charge had had enough. They sold the network. Three years later, it was off the air forever.

The *Queen for a Day* staff with its King, Jack Bailey, early 1960s.

Queen for a Day

"A chamber of horrors." "The worst program on the air." "What hath [NBC chief] Sarnoff wrought?"

That, to the critics, was *Queen for a Day*. Yet for almost 10 years on television and 20 on radio, *Queen* reigned. "It became daytime TV's all-time biggest hit, with 13 million regular viewers watching every day," write Bart Andrews and Brad Dunning in *The Worst TV Shows Ever*.

Every day, host Jack Bailey would step through a purple velvet curtain, look at the viewer, and ask, "Would you like to be queen for a day?" Then Bailey and some lovely model would show off one piece of expensive merchandise after another: "fur coats, dresses, TV sets, washing machines, ad nauseam, while an off-camera announcer extols the wonderful virtues of each," Andrews and Dunning report.

From there, says journalist R. Daniel Foster in *Los Angeles* magazine, "contestants had to earn the sympathy of the audience by reading aloud their often pathetic wishes." One contestant wanted "tires and gasoline to help transport [her] newly adopted blind Chinese toddler to San Francisco for medical treatment—and added that her unemployed husband had broken five ribs in eight places after falling off a ladder." Another contestant said, "I need $100 for a divorce. My husband tried to rape my six-year-old daughter, then left with the money and the car."

The audience would applaud for each contestant. The one who earned the loudest applause (for the most painful story) got wrapped in a luxurious robe, crowned with a tiara, seated on a throne, and handed a bouquet of roses.

Then came the gifts. "A vacation, acres of merchandise and clothing, a picture in the *Hollywood Citizen News*, and a Hollywood whirl that might have included a House of Westmore makeover, an MGM Studios tour, and dinner and dancing at the Trocadero and Cocoanut Grove," writes Foster. Producer Howard Blake said, "The more gifts we gave to the queen, the more money we made" from companies paying *Queen* to display and describe their wares. "Some 5,000 queens wailed their way into the hearts of the program's middle-age audiences, with a total purse exceeding $23 million," Andrews and Dunning report.

Queen eventually went the way of all TV and, in 1964, was canceled. Nevertheless, Foster reports, the Queen Club—an organization of former queens—has been convening since 1947. As Queen Virginia Lovell says, "We were keeping house but not getting credit for it. Being Queen gave us an identity."

Fifteen-minute TV news

From 1948 and the first five-day-a-week network newscast (CBS TV News) to the mid-1960s, 15 minutes was the standard length for the nightly news.

Though short, the shows were serious news operations. And they had wit; reporter Gary Paul Gates wrote in *Air Time: The Inside Story of CBS News*, "When he was reporting on a rather silly debate over whether the name of Boulder Dam should be changed to Hoover Dam, [NBC's David] Brinkley wearily suggested that the way to end the squabble would be to have the former president 'change his name to Herbert Boulder.'"

Still, they had little coverage of science or the arts, or in-depth reporting on any topic. "We're forced to be excessively brief to the point of superficiality," Brinkley complained. "There's no time for background."

CBS proposed a half-hour newscast. "The proposal ran into stiff resistance, particularly from the network's affiliates, which were reluctant to yield the local air time (with its local advertising revenues) that CBS would need," says Gates. "Corporate pressure and cajolery, including financial compensation, eventually brought the affiliates into line.... In August 1963, the regular 15-minute broadcast was turned over to [substitute anchorman] Harry Reasoner and an auxiliary staff while [regular anchor Walter] Cronkite, [producer Don] Hewitt, and their people went into 'rehearsal' for the half-hour show."

On September 2, CBS put its longer newscast on the air. The show offered an interview with President Kennedy, perhaps to reveal what it could do beyond just headlines. It also covered the Tokyo production of the musical *My Fair Lady*, including the song "With a Little Bit of Luck" in Japanese. "The added time made all the difference," said *New York Times* TV critic Jack Gould. "Enough of the number was shown to allow the audience to savor the delicacy of the international stage." NBC premiered its own half-hour news a week later, trumpeted by full-page newspaper ads.

Despite the hype, "both shows were much the same as they had been in the 15-minute form," said Gould days later. "The chief change for the moment seemed to be only more headline bulletins, not any appreciable increase in true depth or diversity of coverage."

Meanwhile, ABC—the youngest, smallest network—hung on to 15-minute news until 1967.

Half-hour newscasts opened the door to today's 24-hour news networks. As NBC news chief Reuven Frank said in 1963, "This is what TV really is designed for. It certainly wasn't made only to save you the price of a movie."

The Arsenio Hall Show

"Woof! Woof! Woof!"

Whirling their fists in the air, the members of Arsenio Hall's audience barked their approval. The raucous noise fit Hall's vision for his show: a party for the off-spring of Johnny Carson's middle-aged *Tonight Show* viewers.

Hall was a Black stand-up comedian (he explained his first name as "Greek for Leroy") who grew up admiring Carson. He was appearing on talk shows in 1987 when Joan Rivers quit her own late-night Fox-network talkfest. Hall took her place and did a creditable job.

He already had a deal with Paramount Pictures to make movies. Paramount's *Star Trek* reruns had shown the studio the power of syndication, and syndicated talk shows (*Oprah*, for example) had shown everyone that they could earn fortunes. The studio was willing to give Hall his own show.

Though he admired Carson, Hall went another way. No desk. No sidekick. A funkier band. A noisier audience.

Hall claimed to have pledged Paramount about 2.5 million viewing house-holds. His first show—January 3, 1989, with Brooke Shields, Luther Vandross, and Leslie Nielsen—delivered more than three million. "*The Arsenio Hall Show* was being seen in 92% of the country on 135 different television stations," says Hall biographer Norman King.

As executive producer as well as host, the 29-year-old Hall had made a talk show for the MTV generation. Arsenio outdrew network offerings such as ABC's long-popular *Nightline* and became the second most popular show in late night, just below Carson.

Critics attacked Hall for softball interviewing, especially with controversial guests such as Minister Louis Farrakhan, but his fawning approach attracted celebrities who shunned other shows. Notoriously shy singer Michael Jackson appeared on *Arsenio*. It was actor Robert De Niro's first talk-show stint.

Arsenio entered public affairs, too. "During the 1992 riots in Los Angeles, Hall was among the first on the streets," wrote *New York Times* editor Veronica Chambers, "and his sensitive, community-based shows sometimes outclassed the local news broadcasts." The show had Bill Clinton, hip in sunglasses, wailing on a saxophone.

Athlete Magic Johnson did *Arsenio* the day after he revealed that he had AIDS; that episode gave the show its highest rating, more than nine million households.

But on May 22, 1992, Carson retired. Jay Leno replaced him. In the fall of '93, David Letterman's *The Late Show* premiered in a time slot that, like Leno's, overlapped Hall's. Leno and Letterman's fierce competition for audiences hurt Hall, especially as Letterman was grabbing Hall's young viewers. By January 1994, Arsenio had lost 24 stations. It had slid to drawing just over two million households.

Hall bowed out. On May 27, 1994, the first Black man to have a top-rated talk show presented his last episode.

Donahue

Phil at his best, stirring up an audience with the Reverend Al Sharpton as his guest, 1988.

Whether he hosted presidential candidates, gay weddings, transvestites (with Phil himself in a skirt), dwarf tossing, interracial lesbian parents, or Nobel laureates, the secret to Phil Donahue's success sat in plain view.

Phil respected the American housewife.

Feminist Gloria Steinem, who frequently appeared on *Donahue*, said, "Phil discovered that women in the daytime are smart. He took their opinion seriously." By so doing, he stayed on the air for nearly 30 years, reached almost nine million people a day, and earned 20 Emmys.

Donahue was co-anchoring local television news and hosting a local radio talk show when George Resing, station manager of WLWD television in Dayton, Ohio, hired him to do talk on TV. Inspired by a small-time syndicated show called *Contact*, which featured a host interviewing a guest and viewers phoning in questions and comments, the first *Phil Donahue Show* aired on November 6, 1967, with atheist Madalyn Murray O'Hair as guest.

"*The Phil Donahue Show* was an overnight hit," wrote journalist Kathy Haley in *Broadcasting* magazine. "By the fall of 1971, 41 stations carried the *Phil Donahue Show*." Eight years later, with more than 200 stations, Phil's was the most popular show in syndicated TV.

Unlike other talk shows, the series (shortened to *Donahue* in 1974) had no band, jokes, or sidekick, and few show-biz celebrities. It covered shocking topics: abortion, incest, child abuse. It featured such serious newsmakers as Ralph Nader

(Donahue's most frequent guest), Salman Rushdie, and Nelson Mandela (in his only talk-show appearance after leaving prison).

But mostly, it had Phil and his audience. Haley writes, "Almost from the first day, audience members would feed Donahue questions to pose to the guest. And the questions, Donahue recalls, 'were great, some of them much better than anything [the staff and I] thought of.'"

Then came *Oprah*. Premiering in 1986, Oprah Winfrey's talk show, following Phil's format, eventually beat *Donahue* in the ratings. The deluge followed: Geraldo Rivera, Montel Williams, Maury Povich, Jenny Jones, Jerry Springer, Ricki Lake, and more. Talk shows fought for the most shocking guests.

By January 1996, Phil had had it. He announced his retirement. With the episode taped on May 2, filled with video clips from his best shows, *Donahue* went off the air.

But its influence remains. As John Henson, host of E! Entertainment Television's talk-show series *Talk Soup*, said, "I've seen Oprah, Sally, Rolonda, Leeza, Geraldo, Maury, Montel, Jerry, and everyone in between. They all have one thing in common: They flow from the River Phil."

MUSIC AND DANCE
78 rpm records

December 7, 1877. John Kryesi, a Thomas Edison employee developing a phonograph, finally gets the device to work. He has invented sound recording.

But not records—at least, not as we think of them. The Edison system used a cylinder. Ten years passed before Emile Berliner, a German immigrant (and not an Edison employee) recorded onto a flat surface.

Since it's easier to stamp audio grooves onto a disc than a cylinder, Berliner's records became the standard. In 1903, operatic tenor Enrico Caruso recorded *Vesti la Giubba* for the Victor Talking Machine Company, the first disc to sell a million copies. In 1912, even Edison quit the cylinder business in favor of discs.

Some shiny, happy 78s.

By 1917, Victor's assets hit $33.2 million. In 1922, says *78 RPM Records and*

Prices by Louisiana State University's Peter Soderbergh, "More than 100 million records are produced, and Americans spend more money on recorded music than on any other mode of entertainment." Two years later, Vernon Dalhart's *Wreck of the Old 97* sold over six million copies, becoming the 78 era's biggest seller.

That speed—78 revolutions per minute on a turntable with a diamond needle picking up the sounds encoded into the grooves—took a while to become the standard. Some of Berliner's early discs spun at 70 rpm, and 78 didn't become fixed as the one and only speed until 1926.

But the 78 had a problem. Each side contained less than five minutes of sound. A symphony, opera, or Broadway show filled several 12-inch discs in a bulky package the size of a photo album.

Record companies tried other formats. In 1930 and '31, engineers working for Victor (by then RCA Victor) develop a 33⅓ rpm record. In spinning more slowly, it could play longer before running out of grooves.

RCA Victor's management did nothing with the new development. After all, 78s were making good money. In 1947, according to Soderbergh, "over 400 million [78 rpm] records sold."

Enter CBS Records engineer Peter Goldmark. In 1948, he and his team developed their own 33⅓ rpm record, which could play for 20 minutes on each side. Goldmark's LP (long-playing) disc became the standard. "By 1957, the 78 rpm disc had been replaced," writes Soderbergh.

If you go into record stores, you'll still see 78 rpm recordings—they're on compact discs. After all, the 78 gave the public Enrico Caruso and Emilia Galli-Curci, Louis Armstrong and Duke Ellington, Frank Sinatra and Bing Crosby, and dozens of others who thrill the world even now.

Ballet Russe

"Cathy adores a minuet, the Ballet Russe, and crepe suzette..."

But Patty loves to rock 'n' roll, as we know. While most teenagers would agree with *The Patty Duke Show*'s all-American Patty, her sophisticated twin cousin Cathy was on to something.

Russian impresario Serge Diaghilev founded the first Ballet Russe (literally, "Russian ballet") in 1909. It presented dancers Anna Pavlova and Vaslav Nijinksy, choreographers Nijinsky and George Balanchine, composers Igor Stravinsky and Maurice Ravel, and set and costume designers Pablo Picasso, Marc Chagall, and Henri Matisse. Rarely has one company hired so many geniuses.

The Ballet Russe was revolutionary. Its performance of Stravinsky's *The Rite of Spring* literally caused a riot. Before Diaghilev, only a few knew about Russian dance; thanks to him, it attained a fame that has continued ever since.

When Diaghilev died in 1929, the Ballet Russe disbanded. But Diaghilev had a contract for shows in Monte Carlo, and Monte Carlo Opera director Raoul Gunsbourg wanted them.

He hired Rene Blum, a top play and operetta director, as director of ballet. Blum teamed with Vasily Voskresensky, a former Russian military officer turned ballet producer calling himself Colonel W. de Basil. The pair gathered some of Diaghilev's people, plus new talent. On January 17, 1932, the Ballet Russe de Monte Carlo gave its first show.

The new Ballet Russe "was one of the balletic success stories of its time," says dance critic Jack Anderson in *The One and Only: The Ballet Russe de Monte Carlo*. "Its repertoire included Diaghilev revivals and ambitious new works." It included great dancers and choreographers such as David Lichine, Leonide Massine, and Tatiana Riabouchinska.

Afternoon of a Faun
by the Ballet Russe.

Blum quit in 1935, angry that de Basil was getting most of the credit for the company's success. Success it certainly had, enough to attract imitators. "In July [1935], a company called the Ballet Russe de Paris [opened]," writes dance critic Kathrine Sorley Walker in *De Basil's Ballets Russes*. Blum, with Massine, built a company first called Ballets de Monte-Carlo and then Ballet Russe de Monte Carlo. Other groups didn't take the Ballet Russe name but copied the dances. De Basil even created his own "copy"—a second Ballet Russe company, which he sent on tour.

De Basil died in 1951. In 1952, his company went under. The Massine-Blum Ballet Russe, meanwhile, kept staging ballets by Balanchine and others.

By 1962, Anderson reports, "the Ballet Russe was not doing as well [in ticket sales] on tour as it once had, and production costs were rising." On April 14, the company performed *Swan Lake* at the Brooklyn Academy of Music. It was the last night of the Ballet Russe.

Eight-track tapes

"That most maligned and ridiculous of all audio formats," *Audio* magazine columnist Corey Greenberg called it. The eight-track tape, once a fixture in American cars, became a symbol of outmoded would-be hipness.

An aviation inventor-tycoon devised the eight-track—engineer Bill Lear, creator of the Lear private jet, a favorite status symbol for corporate chieftains. In 1963, his daughter Shanda picked up Lear from an airport "in a Lincoln Continental that she had borrowed from the son of Earl Muntz, a former used-car dealer and inventor," says journalist Richard Rashke, author of *Stormy Genius: The Story of Aviation's Maverick, Bill Lear*. "Attached to the dashboard was Muntz's new four-track car stereo tape player. Shanda knew her father would be interested in the Muntz Auto-Stereo because of his early work on car radios."

Lear became a distributor of Muntz stereos and—with Sam Auld, his top electronics engineer—tried to create a better model. Muntz's tape cartridge was as big as a dinner plate, the tape snarled, and it had poor sound quality.

Lear and Auld made a smaller cartridge that could play for two hours without rewinding or being turned over. They improved the sound by doubling the number of audio channels ("tracks") on the tape. And they gave it a distinctive package: "a plastic housing that was vibration resistant and would permit play at any angle," according to the rock history *You Really Got Me* by Doug Hinman and Jason Brabazon. Then Lear started making deals.

The eight-track Willie.

"In April 1965," says Rashke, "RCA [Records] promised to offer everything from the Beatles to Beethoven [on eight-tracks], and Ford promised to offer the Lear Stereo Eight in its Lincoln Continental, Ford Galaxie LTD, and Thunderbird." In July 1966, Rashke adds, "[Lear] had a deal with Chrysler to offer add-on [i.e., not built-in] units through Chrysler dealers; he was selling home players through Capitol Records; he had set up a string of 5,000 distributors across the country; and he had talked Sears into featuring his Stereo Eight in its Christmas catalog. Lear was projecting the production of

10,000 players a day by the end of the year and two million cartridges a month."

Little did Lear and others realize that the eight-track's demise was coming. By 1964, the Dutch electronics firm Philips had developed the audiocassette. While the eight-track ruled the United States, cassettes conquered Europe. The cassette—smaller than an eight-track and eventually offering better audio quality—took over America in the 1970s and '80s.

Although obsolete, an eight-track outdoes newer, fancier systems in one way, says audiophile Greenberg. "It reminds me of how much fun listening to music and playing with gear can be when you stop taking it all so seriously."

Grateful Dead concerts

A lot of bands aren't there anymore, but few if any have had the following of the Grateful Dead. Few if any have had concert after concert that was as much tribal gathering as musical performance.

The Dead began in the mid-1960s as the Warlocks, a San Francisco jug band whose members mixed all sorts of musical styles. Garcia later explained where the band got its name. "One day, we were all over at [bassist Phil Lesh's] house.... He had a big Oxford dictionary, I opened it, and there was 'grateful dead,' those words juxtaposed." The phrase came from an ancient Egyptian prayer. "I said, 'How about Grateful Dead?,' and that was it."

The Dead became the band for novelist Ken Kesey and his Merry Pranksters, who threw Acid Test parties featuring the psychedelic drug LSD. Through a series of Bay Area concerts, the band gained considerable popularity. Their house became a part of bus tours of Haight-Ashbury, San Francisco's hippie neighborhood.

None of that mattered nationally. Said Joe Smith, president of the Dead's record label, Warner-Reprise, "We couldn't sell the Grateful Dead's records in a traditional manner.... You couldn't take your ad in *Billboard* and sell a record that way. We found that they had to be seen.... The cult was important. Free concerts where you handed out fruits and nuts were important."

The Dead soon began taking care of those details themselves. In 1967—when

The Dead's Jerry Garcia.

their first album, *The Grateful Dead*, was released—the band and their manager, Rock Scully, set up the Great Northwestern Tour. "They handled everything from tickets to posters to concert security themselves," wrote journalist Steve Chapple and musician–social scientist Reebee Garofalo in *Rock 'n' Roll Is Here to Pay: The History and Politics of the Music Industry*.

Sometimes, the Dead made the wrong choices. In 1970, the band arranged security for a free concert where the Rolling Stones were to play at Altamont Speedway in Northern California. The Dead hired the violent Hell's Angels biker gang, who ended up attacking audience members and killing one of them.

But the band went on, thanks to its fans. A stoned, mellow bunch, many of them followed the band from show to show, turning each performance into a hippie revival.

The Dead became an institution. In 1994, their biggest year (nearly two million admissions), they were voted into the Rock and Roll Hall of Fame. Hall of Fame chief curator John Henke listed the Dead's "Dark Star" and "Uncle John's Band" in a list titled "500 Songs That Shaped Rock." And the Dead were the fifth biggest touring act of 1995, the band's 51 shows attracting more than 1,300,000 people and grossing more than $38 million.

On July 9, 1995, the Dead held what would be its last concert. Soon after, Jerry Garcia died of complications from drug abuse. Rather than replace him, the band decided that it would no longer tour. Thirty years of tribal life were over.

OTHER ENTERTAINMENT
Stereoscopes

"In the days when there was no such entertainment as movies, color-slide projectors, picture magazines, and television, the stereoscope was a popular source of education and good, clean fun in many homes." Thus writes historian Everett Wilson. "When conversation began to lag or when one wanted an excuse to sit close to a friend," Wilson says, it was time to whip out the stereoscope.

It was a simple machine: a double-lensed chamber with a bar sticking out in front of it; at the end of the bar, metal clips held specially made side-by-side, virtually identical photos, called stereographs. When the viewer looked through the lenses, the two flat stereograph images became one image with realistic depth.

English physicist Charles Wheatstone invented an early version of the stereoscope in the 1830s. It didn't work well, since his images were drawings, which didn't have the depth or precision synchronization of photos.

In 1849, Scottish physicist David Brewser created the stereoscope camera. It had two lenses, spaced as far apart as a person's eyes; when one viewed its photos in the stereoscope's lenses, it mimicked the eyes' depth perception.

After Queen Victoria used a stereoscope at a London exhibition and doctor Oliver Wendell Holmes devised an improved stereoscope, the gadget's popularity exploded. "The demand for stereographs grew so rapidly in the United States that the government put a revenue stamp on all stereographic images to help finance the Civil War," wrote *Christian Science Monitor* reporter Leigh Montgomery.

**Care for a look?
A stereoscope set up
for viewing.**

Stereo photographers shot everything. They took news events: the Wright Brothers' flights, the 1904 St. Louis World's Fair, the 1906 San Francisco earthquake, and the battlegrounds of World War I. The Sears Catalog advertised Western scenes ("the young Sioux Indian with his racing pony; the medicine man in his weird incantations"), beautiful sights ("waterfalls and other famous natural phenomena, some of the world's most famous buildings, places of historical interest"), and comedic shots ("laughable hugging and kissing scenes, humorous scenes of domestic tribulations, amusing bathing scenes").

Competition from new media, such as radio, records, and movies, made the once-thrilling stereoscopes less exciting. They played their last important role during World War II, reports Montgomery: "Aerial stereographic views were used during that war as a tool to observe the topography of invasion sites."

The classic stereoscopes went out of business after the war—although a new version, the Viewmaster, lived on as a kid's toy. They had served well, entertaining civilians and training the troops, and they had earned a good rest.

Vaudeville

For almost 50 years, vaudeville was America's favorite entertainment. The stars who worked in it are legends: Fred Astaire, the Marx Brothers, W.C. Fields, Bob Hope, George Burns, George M. Cohan, Mae West, Harry Houdini, Will Rogers, and hundreds more. In his book *After the Ball: Pop Music from Rock to Rap*, musicologist Ian Whitcomb writes, "Vaudeville was an Irish stew of acts that included anything which might attract the public, from one-legged acrobats to John L. Sullivan (the fighter), William Jennings Bryan (the politician), and President McKinley's niece on crutches."

Some say that the name comes from Vau de Vire, a river valley in Normandy known for songs of love, drinking, and satire. Wherever it originated, the name was first used in America by impresario Tony Pastor, who in the early 1880s started offering family-oriented variety shows.

Vaudeville theaters usually offered two shows a day. According to the *Grolier Encyclopedia of Knowledge*, "The typical show opened with an action-packed 'dumb act,' such as acrobats or cyclists, that did not need to be heard while people were coming in. The second spot went to a typical vaudeville act, such as a song-and-dance or comedy team, that performed in front of a curtain while stage hands set up scenery for the production to follow, which might be a musical number or a comedy sketch—something that stressed the show's diversity. The first star came next, and the first half climaxed with an exciting headliner. The second half opened with an act that regained the fun and pace of the show and settled the audience down. Next came a production, often a dramatic scene with a famous actor doing a 'bit' of a play. In the eighth spot on the typical nine-act bill came the biggest star of the show, often a comedy act. The program closed as it opened—with a showy act that left the audience with a sense of action and abundance."

In the early 1930s, the Depression and talking movies hurt vaudeville. The best performers left for radio, film, and Broadway. In the mid-1930s, New York City's Palace Theater, the greatest of all vaudeville houses, stopped presenting vaudeville shows.

There were attempts to bring vaudeville back. In 1949, the Palace put on a new vaudeville show. It didn't last.

In the 1950s, television revived vaudeville, sort of. *The Ed Sullivan Show* and other variety series presented everything from distinguished actors to trained seals. It wasn't the same, though.

Although vaudeville is gone, anyone who watches old movies can see stars and performances that the two-a-day shows honed to a gleam. As long as video stores carry Fields, West, and the Marxes, vaudeville is never truly dead.

Billy Rose Aquacade

Billy Rose thought huge. A songwriter ("Paper Moon," "Me and My Shadow") and Broadway producer (he put an elephant on stage in the hit *Jumbo*), his most famous presentations may have been his Aquacades.

In the mid-1930s, Rose put on a show at Fort Worth's Centennial Fair. At the climax, according to his sister Polly Rose Gottlieb's *Nine Lives of Billy Rose*, "A water lagoon was revealed, and a gondola sailed across with the help of unseen wires and propmen." The crowd loved it. "'If they get so excited over that sliver of water,' Billy asked thoughtfully, 'what do you suppose would happen if I had a massive pool and put a lot of pretty swimmers in it?'"

By 1937, Rose's Fort Worth success prompted Cleveland to invite him to stage a show there. According to Gottlieb, Rose shocked the city fathers, saying, "We've gotta use Canada for our backdrop, the moon and stars for our props, and Lake Erie for our swimming pool...[and] a curtain of water...big spouts covering every inch of the first few feet of the [stage] apron and across the entire stage. I want that water to shoot up 30 feet. And it's gotta dance!"

It did. When it subsided, the curtain revealed "150 aquaboys and aquabelles in shimmering white, skin-tight bathing suits," Gottlieb recalls. "They plunged into the water one at a time, a quarter of a second apart, rippling into Lake Erie like the snap of a long, white leather whip." The show included Olympic champion Johnny Weismuller (the movies' Tarzan).

Two years later, for the New York World's Fair, Rose put on an even grander production. He built a pool more than 270 feet long, plus a brick-and-stone amphitheater. His show included Weissmuller and Gertrude Ederle, the first woman to swim the English Channel. It also had, according to the *New York Times'* Christopher Gray, "lights, singing, dancing, water ballet, synchronized swimming, stunt diving, slapstick and 177 'Aquafemmes.'"

"By August 1939, 2.5 million visitors had paid 25 to 99 cents to see the Aquacade, and Billy Rose was clearing $80,000 a week," according to Gray. In 1940, Olympic swimmer Larry "Buster" Crabbe replaced Weismuller; he too became a movie star, playing Buck Rogers. Rose put an Aquacade in San Francisco, which presented teenage swimmer Esther Williams, who became a movie star herself.

When the Aquacades closed, their New York site became a public swimming pool. The amphitheater was named the Gertrude Ederle Amphitheater.

Rose died in 1966. In 1977, the pool was closed. In 1982, so was the amphitheater.

By the mid-1990s, the Aquacade was a ruin. But the shows had made their way into history as spectacles that few have even tried to duplicate.

all gone

Chapter Five

FADS, TRENDS, AND WAYS OF LIFE

One of the most startling things about fads is not that they fade. Fading is in their nature. It's that they blaze so bright for so short a time.

Phone booth stuffing, for instance, started in South Africa during 1959 and spread to the United States. At Memphis State, 23 students filled a particularly crowded booth. The fad may have found its greatest popularity in California, where the climate was suitably balmy (in more ways than one). But by the year's end, stuffing was over.

Mention the 1960s, and someone is bound to bring up banana peel smoking. Instead of being a favorite pastime for years and years, the trend (a hoax started by the *Berkeley Barb*, an underground newspaper) barely made it out of 1967.

The '70s brought the mood ring. Its heat-sensitive stone changed colors as your emotions raised or lowered your skin temperature. Actress Sophia Loren had one, as did boxer Muhammad Ali, quarterback Joe Namath, and, reportedly, 20 million others—as if they couldn't recognize their own emotions without glancing at a ring. Although the ring returned in the '90s as an item of kitsch, its true heyday was actually quite short.

At the same time, human potential guru Werner Erhard's est—Erhard seminar training—had a nearly decade-long run, hurling enlightenment via verbal abuse ("You people are here today because all of your strategies, your smart-ass theories, and all the rest of your shit hasn't worked for you") at $250 a head. It ended when the abuse triggered lawsuits and the IRS claimed that Erhard owed millions in back taxes.

Some trends last longer, at which point they get called "traditions" or "ways of life." It's an ennobling way to refer to something that can start out just plain silly.

Goldfish swallowing

Lothrop Withington Jr. was a Harvard University freshman with a big mouth. On March 3, 1939, while showing his goldfish-filled aquarium to classmates, Withington boasted that he had swallowed goldfish ever since, as a child, he had seen a Hawaiian do it. One of his pals laid down a $10 bet that Withington couldn't duplicate the stunt.

Withington plucked a three-inch fish from the aquarium, tilted his head back and dropped it, wiggling, into his mouth. "Those present saw the young scholar carefully chew the squirming morsel and swallow every bit of it without regurgitating," report authors Frank Hoffmann and William Bailey in their book *Mind and Society Fads*. As the *Boston Globe* described the event, "There seemed to be some difficulty at first—some internal struggle—but after a brief moment of confusion, the fish eater swallowed, and all was well." He pocketed the 10 bucks. A legend began to spread.

A student at Franklin and Marshall University "swallowed three fish and claimed to put Harvard in its place," Paul Kirchner reports in his book *Forgotten Fads and Fabulous Flops: An Amazing Collection of Goofy Stuff That Seemed Like a Good Idea at the Time*. Harvard student Irving Clark Jr. defended the crimson by gobbling 24 fish. The University of Pennsylvania's Gilbert Hollandaersky ate 25. "Then University of Michigan's Julius Aisner answered with 28, followed by Boston College's Donald V. Mulcahy, who consumed 29," write Hoffmann and Bailey. Jack Smookler of Northeastern University swallowed 36. M.I.T.'s Albert E. Hayes Jr. consumed 42. A Kutztown State Teachers College freshman sucked down 43. Clark University's Joe Deliberato ate a startling 89.

The Boston Animal Rescue League and other animal-protection groups threatened criminal prosecution. Students who didn't swallow goldfish formed Societies for the Prevention of Goldfish Eating. Massachusetts state senator

Donald Mulcahy, dropping one of his 29 goldfish, 1939.

George Krapf proposed a law commanding the state conservation department to save the fish. "The U.S. Public Health Service warned that goldfish might contain tapeworms which, lodging in the intestinal tract, would cause anemia," Hoffmann and Bailey note, adding, "Chicago psychologist Robert N. McMurray called goldfish swallowing the most egregious of exhibitionist acts in which the eater delights in being repulsive."

Students kept downing fish. But less than two months after the fad had begun, it was in decline.

There were attempts at revival. Kirchner says, "Goldfish swallowing made a brief comeback in 1967 at St. Joseph's College in Philadelphia, when one student swallowed 199." But aside from that brief flare-up, the fad had spun itself out.

By the way, the record for goldfish swallowing was set in 1939 by a St. Mary's sophomore—the student consumed 210.

Dance marathons

Fads by the dozen were born in the 1920s. And of them all, "only marathon dancing fever seemed inexhaustible," declares the book *Fads: America's Crazes, Fevers and Fancies* by Peter L. Skolnik, Laura Torbet, and Nikki Smith.

Although dancing mania, a pathological condition, had been around for centuries—the *Guinness Book of World Records* notes an outbreak in 1374 "when hordes of men and women broke into a frenzied dance in the streets which lasted for hours"—organized marathon dances became famous in 1923 when dancer Homer Moorehouse of North Tonawonda, New York, died after 87 hours on the floor.

Moorehouse's fate didn't deter other dancers. In 1928, Hollywood press agent Milton Crandall staged the "Dance Derby of the Century" in Madison Square Garden. With a $5,000 prize at stake and a three-piece band spurring them on, 91 couples began dancing. "Meals were served army-style, dished out of large vats on long tables; dance-floor hair shampoos were arranged; and cots were provided in the separate men's and women's dressing areas for the rest breaks," *Fads* reports. After the first week, the exhausted dancers began to attack each other with punches and kicks.

Exhausted dancers at a marathon in the 1930s.

The event lasted 482 hours—nearly three weeks. It could have gone on longer, says *Fads*: "Only Louis Harris, New York City commissioner of health, was able to have any effect on the proceedings; he simply closed them down."

It didn't matter; other marathons went on. Many a dancer fell asleep in the arms of a partner who continued to drag him or her around the floor. In 1934, dancer (and later movie star) June Havoc set a record for an individual, dancing for an astonishing 3,600 hours. But even she couldn't match the longest marathon ever: 4,152½ hours, running from June 6 to November 30, 1932. The prize was $1,000, less than 25 cents per hour.

The marathons were fun in the madcap atmosphere of the 1920s and cheap entertainment during the Depression. But as the 1930s ended, so did dance marathons.

Yet this most punishing of fads actually came back. From 1973 to 1975, marathon dancing returned—but the new ripple of marathons didn't engulf public attention as the earlier wave did.

Dance marathons have vanished, possibly forever. But as long as there are men and women with more stamina than sense, dance marathons may make another comeback.

Panty raids

1952. A swarm of male students tromps across the campus of the University of Michigan. They storm the doorstep of a women's dorm and demand tribute. From their windows, the women hurl white, frilly fabric: their underwear.

The men accept with glee, and a national fad is on. It strikes Tufts University, Jackson College, Vanderbilt, the University of Illinois. The men loudly beg and chant; they "climb the walls or shinny up drainpipes and actually raid the buildings in search of trophies," recalls University of Kansas English professor Joel J. Gold in *The Chronicle of Higher Education*.

Sometimes, the women tried to deter the hordes by tossing buckets of water onto them; other times, brassieres, hose, slips, and other unmentionables freely flew from dorms and sorority houses. Victorious males hung the spoils of their raids from their own windows, displaying signs emblazoned UNDIE SALE.

Opinions on the raids were mixed. After a raid at the University of Missouri, the state's governor merely murmured, "Boys will be boys."

But on other campuses, according to the history *Our Glorious Century*, "some raids resulted in minor injuries and property damage." At Columbia, a crowd of gleeful, shouting men numbered more than 100 and didn't disperse until the police came. In Gainesville, Florida, at least one young man actually had to be carried from the scene.

By the end of the '50s, the panty raids were over. But many a no-longer-young man remembers them with a smile.

They may not admit it, though. As Joel Gold writes, "When I visited my alma mater a little while ago for a reunion, I tried to bring up [a particular raid] with a number of friends—now lawyers, judges, physicians, professors—who had certainly been on the prowl, and bragging about it, that famous night. Even though the statute of limitations had expired decades ago, however, not one of them could recall leaving the [men's] dorm that evening. Not one had been up on a balcony. Not one had bayed on a sorority-house lawn.

"Loss of memory is a terrible thing. Usually."

The young scholars of Columbia University indulge in some extra-curricular activities, with underwear.

Streaking

You could be anywhere—strolling along a city street, reading in a library, sitting in a football stadium during a game—and suddenly, a flash of flesh runs past, grabbing your eye and startling you into wondering, "Was that guy naked?" You had witnessed a streak.

In 1974, streakers were everywhere: New York's Wall Street; a park in Lima, Ohio; a jet in mid-flight from London to New York; the Michigan and Hawaii legislatures. "They streaked the Lyndon Johnson library, making Lady Bird [Johnson] laugh and Walter Cronkite blush," reports *Fads: America's Crazes, Fevers and Fancies* by Peter L. Skolnik, Laura Torbet, and Nikki Smith. Streaker Robert Opal invaded the Academy Awards behind the elegant David Niven, who quipped, "Isn't it fas-

Streakers on the move at Columbia University.

cinating that probably the only laugh this man will ever get in his life is by stripping off his clothes and showing his shortcomings?"

Primarily, streakers were college students. "At Harvard two streakers, naked except for surgical masks, interrupted a packed amphitheater of students taking a first-year anatomy test," reports *Sports and Recreation Fads*, by Frank Hoffmann and William Bailey. "At Stanford...[streakers] carried golf bags and asked, 'May we play through?' At the University of South Carolina, a streaker entered the library and inquired if *The Naked Ape* were in the collection." Notes *Fads*, "Longest streak honors went to Texas Tech students who skittered about for five hours. The University of Georgia mustered 1,543 students for the largest streak." Streakers hit the University of Southern California, University of Missouri, University of Illinois, Memphis State, Berkeley, Columbia, and even West Point. When colleges held meetings to discuss the problem, the meetings got streaked.

Streakers had a longer history than they knew. In 1688, rakehell Sir Charles Sedley ran through London naked. In 1776, according to Rhode Island Historical Society documents, American soldiers streaked near Brooklyn, New York, "with a design to insult and wound the modesty of female decency."

Like all fads, streaking declined. As the fall of '74 came, bringing cold weather with it, America saw fewer and fewer naked runners.

Although it may no longer be a fad, streaking will probably never vanish entirely. As long as college students take crazy chances to shock the neighbors, you can bet that running naked in public will occur.

Pet rocks

Gary Dahl, a 38-year-old advertising copywriter from Los Gatos, California, is sitting in a bar with a bunch of his pals. They're griping and whining: This one had a dog that peed on the rug, that one's cat ripped the furniture, the other one skipped a vacation because he couldn't find anyone to take care of the family bird.

"I've got no problems with my pet," says Dahl. "I've got a pet rock." Dahl's friends laugh. The craze of 1975 is born.

"[Dahl] got together with a friend, local graphic artist Pat Welsh, who designed an elegant little tan cardboard carrying case, complete with 14 air holes, to package the rocks, which rest inside on a bed of excelsior," wrote *Los Angeles Times* reporter Harriet Stix. He secured $10,000 in start-up funding from George Coakley, head of the advertising agency that employed him.

Lock up your kids! The Pet Rock has escaped from its box.

The key to Dahl's rocks was the 32-page instruction booklet that he wrote and supplied with every box. Dahl told pet owners how to teach their rocks to roll over and play dead ("Rocks love to practice the latter on their own," he said.) "To teach your PET ROCK to FETCH, throw a stick or a ball as far as you can. Next, throw your PET ROCK as far as you can. Rarely, if ever, will your PET ROCK return with the object, but that's the way it goes," Dahl wrote. To teach the rock to attack a mugger, "Reach into your pocket or purse as though you were going to comply with the mugger's demands. Extract your PET ROCK. Shout the command, ATTACK. And bash the mugger's head in."

Dahl promoted his rocks at gift industry retailer shows. He received only 4,800 orders. But the rock began rolling, so to speak, and soon he was shipping up to 6,000 per day at a retail price of $4 apiece. (His instruction book cautioned against finding your own rocks in their natural habitats: "Once a wild rock, always a wild rock.") In all, Dahl's Rock Bottom Productions (his receptionist answered the phone, "You have reached Rock Bottom now") sold more than a million Pet Rocks.

The fad played out, but Dahl returned in 1976 with The Official Sand Breeding Kit, "aimed at all those people who flunked out of the matchbook career offerings ('You too can earn big money…') as upholsterers, truck drivers, motel managers, computer operators, etc.," wrote the *Los Angeles Times'* Jim Houston. And in something of a tribute to the birthplace of the Pet Rock, Dahl opened a saloon, Carry Nation's.

Sand breeding didn't catch on as the Pet Rock did—but it's hard to think that Dahl is too unhappy about it. How often can a man expect to become a millionaire from stuff that's lying around everywhere?

The shame of divorce

In the 1950s, many Americans shunned the divorced. Upstanding, moral people simply didn't get divorced, the reasoning went. Two-time presidential candidate Adlai Stevenson was divorced, and a number of people added that fact into their decision to vote against him.

"Divorce was legal in almost all the states of the Union, but it carried a social stigma," wrote *Smithsonian* magazine's Robert Wernick. "Nice people did not do it, and in most jurisdictions the breaking of a marriage was deliberately made a slow, costly, and embarrassing process."

THE DIVORCEE:
Was promiscuity her only way out of loneliness?

She's tawdry, seamy, and just plain bad. "THE DIVORCEE: Was promiscuity her only way out of loneliness?"

Women in particular were stigmatized. Not only were divorcees seen as a bit slutty, but many women had grown up expecting only to be wives. They had few skills that could earn a living outside the home, and divorce would have left them feeling like failures or worse.

The opposition to divorce went back a long way. It was part of religious law stretching back for centuries. It was also part of the legal system. Even as late as the 1940s, writes author Glenda Riley in *Divorce: An American Tradition*, "South Carolina prohibited divorce, while New York law recognized the sole ground of adultery."

The semi-frontier state of Nevada became the place to go for a divorce. "If you had lived within its borders for six months, you could walk into a courthouse, explain to a judge in private that your spouse had made life unbearable for you and walk out free as a bird," says Wernick. The city of Reno turned divorce into a major industry, creating "divorce ranches" where people could spend their six months in privacy and comfort. Meanwhile, reporters haunted the courthouses for famous faces.

In the mid-1960s, women were starting to emancipate themselves and became less tolerant of intolerable marriages. Moreover, the laws making divorce especially agonizing were starting to loosen. "Beginning with the 1971 case of

Boddie vs. *Connecticut*, United States Supreme Court justices ruled that divorce was a person's fundamental right," says Riley. Divorce grew more common ("Broad swaths of the middle class—not to mention role models at the top of entertainment, business, government, media—have themselves been divorced," wrote *Newsweek*'s Jonathan Alter and Pat Wingert), making the stigma and scandal pale even more.

"The last Reno divorce to merit headlines and pictures in national magazines was that of Mary Rockefeller in 1962," says Wernick. Divorce was still sad, but no longer shameful.

all gone

Chapter Six
FOOD AND DRINK

Styles in food pass like styles in clothes, and food for kids is especially fickle.

Kellogg's Pep and Krumbles: They were whole wheat when whole wheat wasn't cool.

Pillsbury's Funny Face drink mixes were popular in the '60s, but try finding them now. M&M/Mars used to make tan M&Ms, but no longer; the flashier red and blue have taken their place. Kellogg's Pep whole wheat flakes and Krumbles whole wheat shreds were popular for decades, but the company has replaced them with brands such as All-Bran and Frosted Mini-Wheats.

Among nostalgia-cereal collectors—quite a dedicated bunch they are—one of the most popular brands is Quaker Oats' Quisp and Quake. Quisp was an alien with a propeller beanie atop his head, while Quake was a manly, muscular miner. Quaker Oats promoted their cereals by sponsoring a "Which is better, Quisp or Quake?" contest. The characters were created by Jay Ward, the master cartoonist behind Rocky and Bullwinkle, and cels from his animated commercials for the characters sell for hundreds of dollars. While Quake is retired, Quisp may actually come back; Quaker Oats has test-marketed a revived Quisp cereal in some parts of the country.

Not all foods that pass away are intended only for kids, of course. For example, the Pepsi-Cola Company introduced two sodas in the '70s, Aspen and Pepsi Lite. Although the drinks had devoted fans, they were both discontinued due to weak sales. (And, of course, many an adult has enjoyed tan M&Ms and Kellogg's Krumbles—and may even have sneaked a sip of the Funny Face flavor Goofy Grape.)

Cyclamate-sweetened foods

Cyclamate sweetened soft drinks and caused cancer—or did it?

Michael Sveda, a University of Illinois doctoral student in chemistry, had a bad habit: he smoked. In 1937, "he was conducting experiments on sulfamic acid and its salts, and noticed a sweet taste on a cigarette that had touched his laboratory bench," writes the Massachusetts Department of Commerce and Economic Development's Linda Cummings in the anthology *Consuming Fears: The Politics of Product Risks*. "From the 20 compounds with which he was working at the time, Sveda identified the sweetener as sodium cyclohexyl-sulfamate, or cyclamate."

Sveda patented his discovery and assigned it to DuPont, which did nothing with it. Cyclamate was considered an over-the-counter drug, and DuPont didn't deal much in drugs. Abbott Laboratories did, though. DuPont licensed cyclamate to Abbott, which started marketing cyclamate in the mid-1950s—but not as a drug. It was a food sweetener for people with medical conditions that forced them to cut back on sugar.

Thirty times sweeter than sugar, without the bitter aftertaste of saccharin (the other major artificial sweetener), cyclamate soon was everywhere, especially in soft drinks, diet foods, and the sugar substitute Sweet'n Low. "By the late 1960s, cyclamate was an ingredient in over 250 products," says Cummings. "Consumption in 1969 had reached 18.5 million pounds per year, with a retail value of $1 billion."

Anything that big will attract scrutiny. To fend off trouble, Abbott conducted its own study. Unfortunately for Abbott, writes *Reason* magazine's Jacob Kramer, "rats who were fed high doses of the sweetener developed cancer." The Food and Drug Administration took notice and on October 18, 1969, banned cyclamate.

The ban was controversial. Abbott had fed more cyclamate to the rats than any human would consume, so many people thought it foolish to ban cyclamate based on Abbott's study. Moreover, says Kramer, "the World Health Organization, the U.N. Joint Committee on Food Additives, and the National Academy of Sciences have since rejected that study as a fluke because its results could not be reproduced." (Some experts did acknowledge that while cyclamate might be harmless on its own, it might also promote cancer if combined with other substances.)

Despite the controversy, the ban remained in place. Saccharin took cyclamate's place—ironically so, since saccharin is considered more carcinogenic than cyclamate. And although saccharin is still found in Sweet'n Low, most sugar-free products are now sweetened with aspartame.

Abbott Laboratories is trying to get the FDA to rescind the ban on cyclamate. At this writing, it has had no success.

Billy Beer

Presidential brothers sometimes embarrass their siblings. Jimmy Carter's brother, for example, was considered a bumpkin with a beer can protruding from his mouth.

Billy Carter capitalized on his fame (or infamy) in 1977, when Falls City Brewing Company in Louisville, Kentucky, began making Billy Beer. The label (in patriotic red, white, and blue) told the story: "Brewed expressly for and with the personal approval of one of America's great beer drinkers—Billy Carter." It included a photograph of Carter and his autographed tribute:

> **I had this beer brewed up just for me.**
> **I think it's the best I've ever tasted.**
> **And I've tasted a lot.**
> **I think you'll like it, too.**

Said Falls City president Jim Tate, "[My staff] made about five different trial brews, completely different from our two present brews, and [Billy Carter] came and on a blind test said, 'That's the one I want.'" Carter took what the *Wall Street Journal* called "a fat fee" for putting his name on the brew.

He was apparently worth the money. Falls City declared that its profits in 1977 were due solely to Billy Beer. It was sold in 10 states; brewers in Texas, Minnesota, and New York bought licenses to make it. Plus, says writer Paul Kirchner in *Forgotten Fads and Fabulous Flops*, Billy Beer "profited from the 1970s' beer-can collecting craze, as every collector put aside a few six-packs, confident that it would soon disappear and that cans of it would prove to be a good investment."

In 1978, Billy Carter announced that he was an alcoholic. Linked to a man whose drinking was suddenly a serious problem, Billy Beer suffered a falloff in sales. Falls River canceled the brand. It didn't even become a collector's item, says Kirchner: "Billy cans are so common that they've been handed out for free at can collectors' conventions as a publicity stunt."

As presidential embarrassments go, Billy Beer wasn't all that bad. It wasn't a national scandal, it was implicated in no crimes; it was just a not terribly distinguished beer. And as any beer drinker knows, there's no shortage of that.

NOT QUITE GONE, BUT MIGHTY SCARCE
Black Jack chewing gum

Almost everyone has chewed gum. Among the first gums were tree resins; 1,500 years ago, the Mayans chewed *tsitcle*—their word for the milky resin of Latin America's sapodilla tree. In fact, writes pop-culture journalist Robert Hendrickson in *The Great American Chewing Gum Book*, "tsictle became our [word] chicle."

And from that same chicle, sapodilla resin, Thomas Adams made the first modern chewing gum in 1871.

There had been chewing gums before. Former seaman John Curtis created the first commercial chewing gum, a spruce resin, in 1848. "By 1852, the Curtis Chewing Gum Company of Portland, Maine, employed over 200 in its new, three-story factory," reports *The Whole Pop Catalog*. Unlike modern gums, spruce resin was not sweet—Hendrickson calls it woodsy, pungent, and tangy—and it was hard to chew. Adams changed all of that. In 1871, he took out the first patent on a gum-making machine.

Adams used chicle, not spruce. Chicle, says Hendrickson, chews better than spruce. But, he adds, "chicle, chewed neat, tastes like nothing so much as chewed-out chewing gum." So Adams added flavor: "He tried sassafrass first and then shredded licorice," Hendrickson says.

Licorice—"traditionally used for soothing minor throat irritations," according to gum company Warner-Lambert—was a winner. Adams called the resulting gum Black Jack.

**Black Jack and its
old pals in 1993.**

Adams sold Black Jack in pharmacies and vending machines, and made a fortune. Other brands were added. Black Jack, the first mass-produced flavored chewing gum, stayed on the market for a century, a staple of the business.

By the 1970s, dozens of gum brands were available, with flavors that Adams had never imagined. Sales of Black Jack were slow. Warner-Lambert, which by then owned Black Jack, took it off the market.

But not for long. In October 1986, Warner-Lambert created a "Nostalgia Gums Program" to revive Black Jack and two other old, discontinued brands, Clove and Beeman's.

Warner-Lambert discontinued them in 1990, but demand remained high. Nostalgia Gums product manager Tracey Bell said in 1993, "There are many months that we receive over 100 letters from loyal nostalgia gum chewers asking us when the next promotion will be because their 1990 stockpiles are running out." That year, Warner-Lambert revived the brands again.

Although Black Jack's devoted fans can still find it in some stores, it is currently not being produced and distributed. But someday, Warner-Lambert may return Thomas Adams' licorice chicle to America's store shelves.

all gone

Chapter Seven
KIDS' STUFF

Most children's toys that were at any time popular have stuck around, because nostalgic parents have wanted their kids to have the same fun that they themselves had. Even items that have had their troubles—Erector sets were apparently off the market for a while—have come back.

Others, however…

Decoders were wonderful. Sometimes they were embedded in finger rings, sometimes in handheld discs, but either way, kids loved them. The radio adventures of Captain Midnight or Little Orphan Annie often included secret messages—but you could decode them if you had sent away (enclosing money or box tops or some other valuable item) for the decoder! A few manufacturers may still make decoders, but they're clearly nowhere near as common as they used to be.

The same can be said for balsa-wood model airplanes. They could be as long as a boy's torso, and many a kid spent hours painstakingly cutting the wood into the shapes of wings and hulls, gluing together the fragile skeleton, and painting the finished model with the proper military-aircraft colors. The model kits still exist, but not primarily as kids toys; they're part of the world of adult hobbyists.

Some toys, especially dolls, over time become valuable collectors' items. For example, the Kewpie doll, first designed in 1912 by American illustrator Rose O'Neill—who fashioned the doll after her baby brother—were all the rage between 1912 and 1920. Known by their signature tuft of hair, millions of the dolls were sold. Most of the authentic dolls, which have not been manufactured for decades, are now found in antique shops or owned by collectors—and are sold for an average of $150 to $300.

Some toys, while popular, weren't quite so charming. Matchbox Toys made a doll based on Freddy Krueger, the villain of the 1980s' *Nightmare on Elm Street* movie series. Parents groups objected to such a sinister figure, and in 1989 Matchbox killed him. In 1994, the same kind of objections may have helped to cancel the violent Night Trap, a Sega video game that featured women being abducted.

Other toys weren't just tasteless; they were downright dangerous. In 1970, under public pressure, the FDA banned toy cap pistols louder than 138 decibels, a noise as big as a jet engine's, close to the threshold of pain. Toy makers didn't want to do it—they'd been making caps up to 100 times that loud, capable of deafening kids—but they obeyed. Cap pistols are still around, but the old, deafening ones are gone.

The feds also moved against lawn darts, marketed under the name Jarts, because they considered the toys' sharp points dangerous. In 1970, they simply forced Jarts' manufacturer to sell the item not as a toy but as fun for adults, with a label warning against use by children. In 1989, the government finally banned the toy entirely.

Most kids' items that have vanished weren't so sinister. Like decoder rings, they simply went off the market. But that doesn't stop parents from going to toy stores and trying to buy them for Junior.

A fight among the tiny.

Lead toy soldiers

The sweep of history, the drama of battle, the glow of fine craftsmanship—all on a table. That's the appeal of toy soldiers.

"The earliest-known model soldiers date back to ancient Egypt, when complete companies of miniature archers and spearmen carved from wood were buried with their royal commander," writes *GQ* magazine's Stephen Forman. Soldiers of lead existed as far back as ancient Rome.

But the metal soldiers that populated the toy chest of almost every boy in the Western world didn't appear until the mid-1700s. Pewter workers in Nuremberg, Germany, took breaks from making kitchenware to create flat *zinnfiguren*—tin figures—for their children from spare bits of tin and lead. "The enterprising

Johann Gottfried Hilpert, however, is the earliest identified smith to embark upon their commercial manufacture, and by 1770 *zinnfiguren* marched steadily from his thriving Nuremberg workshop into the nurseries of Europe," wrote journalist Barrymore Scherer in *Town & Country* magazine.

Although the German soldiers were popular, it took an Englishman to make them a staple. "In 1893, William Britain, the son of a British toy manufacturer, invented the process of hollow-casting [molding a rounded, detailed, hollow figure] in lead and thereby initiated a toy-soldier revolution," says collector Norman Joplin in *Identifying Toy Soldiers: The New Compact Study Guide and Identifier.*

Generally two to three inches tall, the creations of Britain and his imitators sold in the millions. "Eventually, [they] included representatives of all the military and naval forces of the British Empire and later the Commonwealth, as well as foreign and American armed forces," wrote Scherer. For more than 50 years, boys envisioned themselves as godlike generals manipulating the fate of armies.

The years after World War II were bad for toy soldiers. In England, which dominated the trade, lead was scarce. In the 1960s, many parents, troubled by the Vietnam War, didn't want to buy their children war toys.

A greater concern, though, was that lead is poisonous. In 1966, the British government outlawed the manufacture of the little men. The ban helped to slow the sales of toy soldiers even outside the U.K.

Today, lead soldiers are the province of collectors. A single soldier can sell for thousands of dollars. *Forbes* magazine publisher Malcolm Forbes put 12,000 pieces from his collection on display in New York; he also established the 70,000-piece Forbes Magazine Museum of Military Miniatures in Tangier, Morocco.

The toy soldier, who never flinched from battle, served generations of young boys. At ease, soldier: You're retired.

Eight Crayola colors

Your kids are drawing with Crayolas in a coloring book, just as you did. On a page showing a bowl of fruit, they want to fill in a lemon, just as you did. But if they reach for a lemon-yellow Crayola, just as you did, they won't find it. That color is gone, along with maize, orange-red, raw umber, green-blue, orange-yellow, blue-gray, and violet-blue.

**The last flare-up of
the canceled colors.**

Seven of the colors first appeared when Crayola launched a 48-color set of crayons in 1949 (up from the eight colors that it introduced in 1903). In 1958, when Crayola upped its crew to 64 colors, raw umber joined the gang.

The Crayola Eight were still on the job well into 1990. But market research was catching up with the Eight. Binney and Smith, Crayola's parent company, found that kids wanted brighter colors.

In August 1990, Crayola retired the Eight to the company's Hall of Fame and replaced them with teal blue, jungle green, cerulean, wild strawberry, vivid tangerine, dandelion, royal purple, and fuchsia. And that was that.

Except that it wasn't. *Life* magazine printed a two-page spread in which kids "scurried to use the old colors one last time" (although some kids preferred the new hues). Adults jumped in, too. "A small knot of protesters picketed the company's headquarters, carrying signs like WE TAKE UMBERAGE and SAVE LEMON YELLOW, says the Berkeley Pop Art Project's *Whole Pop Catalog*. A Crayola fact sheet adds, "Groups included RUMPS: the Raw Umber and Maize Preservation Society, CRAYON: the Committee to Reestablish All Your Old Norms and the National Campaign to Save Lemon Yellow."

Cynics may suspect that the company engineered at least some of these protests as a publicity stunt. In any event, Crayola marketing communications specialist Patrick Morris writes, "There was such public outcry among adults that we re-issued those colors for a limited time in a special collectors' tin available until January 1992."

It was the last burst of lemon yellow and its partners. They are the only colors that Crayola has formally retired (except for blue ribbon, made in a limited run to celebrate Crayola's manufacture of its 100 billionth crayon in July 1996). Crayola has announced no plans to retire other colors, although one wonders how well today's children respond to shades such as periwinkle and thistle.

And if your kids need to color in a lemon? Well, there's still laser lemon, unmellow yellow, and of course, a survivor from 1903: plain, un-adjectived yellow.

Heathkits

In the early 1920s, Ed Heath was a barnstorming pilot. As the decade wore on, Heath and other daredevil flyers found less work. He started a company to sell a kit of parts from which hobbyists could build their own airplanes.

Heath died in a crash while testing a new plane. Investor Howard Anthony stepped in, took over, and included a line of aircraft radios.

A legacy began. The Heath Company made kits for radios, stereo record players, computers, and other electronic products.

"We all cut our teeth on Heathkits," said Lee Felsenstein, a computer pioneer who was allied with the Homebrew Computer Club, the spawning ground of Apple Computer and other Silicon Valley empires. Cybergeeks weren't the kits' only fans; Senator Barry Goldwater "used to fly to Heath's headquarters…twice a year in his private plane to buy kits," reports the *New York Times*' Lawrence Fisher.

Eventually, Heath offered hundreds of kits. "Each kit supplied a complete set of parts, including all metalwork and cabinets, with detailed assembly drawings and step-by-step instructions," wrote Julian Hirsch, *Stereo Review*'s "Technical Talk" columnist. Moreover, a machine built from a Heathkit cost almost a third less than one bought in a store.

And it worked just as well. The company's motto was "We won't let you fail," and it didn't. Heath offered help by phone or in its stores. "Most Heathkits worked the first time they were turned on and kept working for many years," Fisher reported.

The young men who learned electronics on Heathkits helped to doom the products. "The personal computer revolution was in some ways a death blow to Heathkits because it siphoned off the most enthusiastic kit builders," Fisher reports. Boys who liked electronics turned to computer hacking, not hi-fi assembly.

There was also the rise of the integrated circuit, which put several components on one chip. It lowered the cost of building machines in a factory, eliminating Heathkits' price advantage. Besides, building your own devices with integrated circuits wasn't as challenging or fascinating as wiring and soldering.

In 1992, Heath closed its kits. The company was already making home-improvement products and educational materials, and it concentrated its efforts there.

But as Heathkit builder Gary Staton has said, "Every kid should try picking up a little soldering pencil, smelling the smoke in the room, and running the wire from point A to point B…. When you're doing it and it works, there's no competition from the assembly-line products."

"Build your own hi-fi" the Heathkit way.

all gone

Chapter Eight

LAW, GOVERNMENT, AND POLITICS

"The good old days weren't always good," Billy Joel sang in "Keeping the Faith." Nowhere is that more true than in the annals of government. Our elected officials and unelected ones have perpetrated some disasters that we can be glad aren't there anymore. (Hey, nobody said nostalgia had to be pretty.)

The Atomic Energy Commission (AEC), for example, conducted nuclear tests that exposed American citizens to dangerously high levels of radiation without their knowledge. The AEC was a key player in the ruin of Robert Oppenheimer, a father of the atomic bomb later unfairly ostracized for holding traitorous views. It was dissolved in 1975 and replaced by the Nuclear Regulatory Commission.

Today, when the media encourages condom use, it may seem odd that Americans could be arrested for using contraception—but from 1873 until the 1970s, that was the case. In 1914 a crusade was begun by Nurse Margaret Sanger, who wrote a pro-contraception book and opened birth control clinics, facing arrest and obscenity charges. Following the FDA's approval of the birth control pill in 1960, a series of court decisions finally made contraception legal.

Then there were poll taxes. In some states, the fee levied on voters was used to keep poor African-

Mr. Jefferson's bill.

88

Americans from voting. In 1964, the 24th Amendment to the Constitution outlawed the poll tax as a part of federal elections.

Other actions by government are more benign. Indian-head nickels and Mercury dimes are lovely to see, but no longer minted. Two-dollar bills, though still in use, are rare in most parts of the United States.

Political groups come and go fast. U.S. history is littered with parties that made a big splash and then subsided—Dixiecrats, Peace and Freedom, American Independent, Progressive, Socialist (running as a Progressive with Socialist support, Senator Robert La Follette took nearly five million votes in the presidential election of 1924), and many more.

SNCC leader Stokely Carmichael shows followers where to stage their sit-in, 1967.

Other groups weren't exactly parties but affected politics nonetheless. The Youth International Party (Yippies) called itself a political party, but it was actually a parody of one. Leftists Jerry Rubin and Abbie Hoffman launched it to make well-publicized fun of the parties in power. "The Yippie strategy was used to great effect during the Festival of Life held outside the 1968 Democratic National Convention in Chicago, when a pig called Pigasus was nominated as the Yippie presidential candidate," says John Button, author of *The Radicalism Handbook: Radical Activists, Groups and Movements of the Twentieth Century*. "The Yippie movement subsided shortly thereafter, but an organization called the Yippies continued to publish protest material for almost 20 more years."

More serious was the Student Non-Violent Coordinating Committee. The SNCC was born during 1960 to help the antisegregation protests occurring in the South. The SNCC went on to organize "freedom rides," in which activists traveled to aid protesters who were running into trouble. The group continued to fight discrimination, but new leaders such as Stokely Carmichael abandoned nonviolence and formed an alliance with the militant Black Panthers, moves that alienated some of the group's most active members. By the early 1970s, the SNCC had dissolved.

This is one of the few sections of this book that departs the United States to delve into events in other countries. This is partly because American culture, for good or ill, already pervades the world. But some foreign events—such as the decline of Nazism in Germany—can't be overlooked even by the most tunnel-visioned American.

Benign or not, political activity is part of our culture. The activities and organizations that aren't there anymore deserve to be remembered.

POLICIES AND INSTITUTIONS
Horse cavalry

"Maudie, it's all over. Them Apaches'll come roarin' over that rise any minute, and you an' I can't hold 'em off alone."

"We ain't alone, Abe. Hear them hoofbeats? The cavalry's comin'!"

Teddy Roosevelt with the Rough Riders, readying to ride.

Since the Turks developed saddles and reins around 1200 B.C., horseback soldiers were a part of war. Hannibal fought the Romans on horse and elephant, and the Romans beat him by using better cavalry than he had. The Mongols invaded Europe on horses in the 1200s, and ruled from Germany to the Pacific.

But cavalrymen, sitting high on horseback, made ideal targets for archers. For protection, both men and horses wore armor. It made them safe but sluggish and clumsy.

Guns, though, could blow even an armored man away. Armies abandoned armor but not horses. Cavalry helped Napoleon on his conquests. In America, horsemen fought in the Civil War and battled Indians.

Again, new inventions changed the cavalry. Barbed wire and fast-firing Gatling guns could sweep across a cavalry charge and cut it down. Cavalrymen switched from charges to less predictable tactics, such as scouting and raiding.

But in World War I, soldiers in Jeeps, tanks, and planes could outrun and outgun horsemen. Despite occasional successes in Palestine and Eastern Europe, cavalry waned.

In World War II, only the Russians and Chinese used cavalry much. "The only American outfit to fight on horseback during World War II was the 26th Cavalry, Philippine Scouts," writes military historian Gregory Urwin in *The United States Cavalry: An Illustrated History*. "When Bataan was surrendered on 9 April 1942, the 26th was one of the few units that had not been broken and was still keeping the Japanese at bay."

In 1950, the United States shut the cavalry down. Other nations had already retired theirs or were doing so, although China used horsemen in the Korean War and even afterwards.

The cavalry wasn't forgotten. Well into the '80s, the U.S. Horse Cavalry Association, composed mostly of cavalry veterans, met to swap memories and re-enact battles. And mechanized cavalry remains a part of warfare.

Urwin writes, "The dash and spirit of the pony soldier lived on among the Army's Armored Force in the person of Lieutenant General George S. Patton, a former colonel of the 3rd and 5th [Horse] Cavalry. He taught his tankers a pair of dicta, which he had coined during his days with the horse cavalry: 'Get around if you can't get through,' and 'The secret of success in mounted operations is to grab the enemy by the nose and kick him in the pants.' Whether they ride today in tanks or helicopters, that elan is still shared by the troopers of the U.S. Cavalry."

HUAC members (including Richard Nixon, left) on the job.

HUAC

Are you now or have you ever been a member of the Communist Party? Answer up, and name your fellow Reds while you're at it. And no back talk like "What if I am? It's none of your business."

That was the tone of the House [of Representatives] Un-American Activities Committee, or HUAC. For nearly 40 years, it investigated people who were alleged subversives.

First proposed in 1930 to investigate communists and fascists, HUAC was turned into a national headline grabber by member Martin Dies. While un-American activities can come from any political view, Dies—who saw little difference between liberals and communists—

focused on the left. His committee accused labor unions of communist control and claimed that liberal politicians were helping communism gain power. He even accepted a witness who accused six-year-old Shirley Temple of being a red dupe.

Temple wasn't the only celebrity to interest the committee. In 1940, '47, and '51, it questioned James Cagney, Gary Cooper, Walt Disney, Ronald Reagan, and Humphrey Bogart, among others. A group of writers—the Hollywood Ten—refused to answer HUAC's queries, and were jailed. Others, including prominent directors and performers, were blacklisted from movie work.

Dies died in 1945, but HUAC went on. Chairmen such as the vitriolic John Rankin (who called anti-HUAC columnist Walter Winchell a "slime mongering kike") continued to attack Reds, aided by young congressman Richard Nixon.

In one of Nixon's triumphs, HUAC, in 1948, accused State Department official Alger Hiss of being a communist. Hiss denied it and was jailed for lying to the committee. The case helped propel Nixon to national prominence.

HUAC remained strong—"by 1960," according to *The Encyclopedia of the United States Congress*, "it had a permanent staff of 49 and an annual appropriation of more than $300,000"—but anticommunist investigations by Senator Joseph McCarthy and the Internal Security Subcommittee of the Senate Judiciary Committee took the spotlight from HUAC, and McCarthy's downfall made Red-hunting disreputable. What's more, says Nixon biographer Fawn Brodie, HUAC was inept: "More than half of the HUAC witnesses whose cases resulted in indictments by grand juries were finally acquitted."

In the 1960s, HUAC examined the Ku Klux Klan and the antiwar movement, but it got little public respect. A 1969 name change to the House Committee on Internal Security didn't help. As Brodie says, "HUAC members abandoned traditional Anglo-American concepts of criminal justice, assumed guilt rather than innocence, and conducted most of their questioning with the assumption that to believe in communism was a crime." In 1975, the House abolished HUAC.

WIN buttons

In 1974, inflation in America was running at nearly 12 percent per year. Many Americans could barely afford necessities.

To fix the problem, President Gerald Ford gathered some of the top minds in money at an economic summit and asked them to find solutions. From the summit came one of the best-intentioned, most-caricatured presidential proposals.

Ford chief of staff Robert Hartmann said in his memoirs, "'WIN' was sort of Siamese twins, one fathered by William J. Meyer, president of the Central Automatic Sprinkler company in Pennsylvania, and the other mothered by Sylvia Porter, the popular financial writer." Meyer wanted a new version of 1933's National Recovery Act, which exhorted businesses to fight the Depression by voluntary acts such as extra hiring. Porter advocated "a nationwide campaign to reduce waste and lower consumer pressure on prices through victory gardens, recycling of paper, cans, and bottles, and voluntary energy conservation."

On October 8, Ford spoke before Congress, wearing a red button bearing the white-lettered word WIN. It stood for Whip Inflation Now, the name of Ford's program. According to Ford, Americans should consume a little less; businesses suddenly deprived of consumer dollars would entice them back by lowering prices, thus curbing inflation.

Millions of Americans liked the idea. The Ford administration ordered up 12 million WIN buttons; nonetheless, Hartmann noted, "we could never keep up the demand." Although inflation did dip a tad.

But some columnists, noted commentator Nicholas Von Hoffman, considered WIN "demented asininity." "Their liberal cartoonist counterparts came up with starving black children eating WIN buttons as their scathing commentary," Hartmann added.

WIN didn't get full support even from Ford's own troops. Administration economist William Simon later said, "Every time the WIN issue came up, we at the Economic Policy Board would hide our heads in embarrassment." Besides, America's unemployment rate topped 7 percent and made some officials worry more about recession than inflation.

The WIN program never died. "It just sort of melted with the winter snow," Hartmann recalled. Other concerns, such as the 1976 presidential election, took precedence.

After Ford left the White House, inflation rebounded. New president Jimmy Carter couldn't cut it down much. In that sense, the WIN campaign had the last laugh.

Gasoline rationing

"Is this trip really necessary?" It was a slogan of World War II. A country drive was unpatriotic when the military needed petroleum for tanks, Jeeps, aircraft, and ships.

Actually, petroleum wasn't very scarce; rubber was. (The Japanese had taken some of the islands that supplied much of America's rubber.) To prevent people from driving too much, wearing out their tires and buying more, the government's War Production Board—formed in 1942 to oversee rationing of all sorts of goods—began rationing gas.

Applicants lined up for a variety of ration cards, note nostalgia writers Robert Heide and John Gilman in *Home Front America: Popular Culture of the World War II Era*. "The categories included: A, non-essential for war driving [limited to only a few gallons per week]; B, for commuters who drive to work but do not use their vehicles on the job; C, salesmen and delivery driving—work related; E, emergency vehicles which included clergy, police, firemen, press photographers, and journalists; T, truckers, work related; X, congressmen. This X category required no rationing at all and naturally brought widespread criticism."

After the war, rationing ended. Americans hit the road and needed more and more gas. But in the 1970s, the Organization of Petroleum Exporting Countries (OPEC) raised oil prices. "From 1970 to 1973, the price of crude oil doubled," says Bondi. "Then, during the October 1973 Arab–Israeli war, the Arab states of OPEC initiated an embargo against Israel's Western allies, including the United States." Gas became scarce, and in 1973, the federal government designed a new rationing system.

The system never went to work. In March 1974, Arab–Israeli peace talks were going well enough that the Arabs lifted the embargo, and gasoline was available again.

In 1979, the Iranians installed the anti-American Ayatollah Ruhollah Khomeini as their leader, and they ceased exporting oil. Other OPEC nations raised their prices. Soon, California instituted a rationing program that allowed citizens to buy gas only every other day, resulting in long lines at gas stations. The next year, President Jimmy Carter set up his own program, to start "if a 20% shortage of oil supplies existed or was likely to exist for 30 days," according to *Facts on File News Digest*.

Fortunately, that condition was never realized. Within another year, the Middle East situation changed, and gasoline abundance returned to the United States.

But if the United States finds more trouble overseas, Americans may again line up to get a few gallons at a time.

POLITICKING AND CAMPAIGNING
Torchlight parades

In the early 1960s, Harry Truman remembered one. "Grover Cleveland ran against Benjamin Harrison in 1892, and when he was elected, my father...rode a gray horse and carried a torch in a torchlight parade, and so did everybody else in town."

Torchlight parades, an election-year ritual, were a fabulous sight. Hundreds or even thousands of people marched, waving American flags and campaign banners, and singing campaign songs.

Torches weren't just for elections, of course. When victorious soldiers came home from a war, they usually got a parade, sometimes a torchlit one.

Torchlight parades had their dangers. In 1912, nine-year-old Stillman Hobbs joined a torchlight parade to celebrate the election of President Woodrow Wilson. "When we were two-thirds of the way along, I noticed my uncle furiously beating at his clothing. At first, I thought he was cold. Then I saw smoke puffing out of the wool coat he was wearing. It had been set afire by sparks from the torches.... His corduroy jacket and trousers underneath were also smoldering.... We found our way to a watering trough at a house nearby. On that chilly November night, the water was covered with a thin skim of ice. Nevertheless, we broke the ice and immersed the victim, smoldering corduroy suit and all."

One of the most famous torchlight parades wasn't American. Staged by propagandist Joseph Goebbels, it took place in Berlin on January 30, 1933, to celebrate Adolf Hitler's ascension to Chancellor of Germany. "Carrying torches, [Nazi] storm troopers started from the Tiergarten at dusk, joined by thousands of Stahlhelm ['Steel Helmet,' a super-patriotic war veterans group] men and passed under the Brandenburg Gate in disciplined columns to the blare of martial music," writes Hitler biographer John Toland. "Hour after hour, they marched down the Wilhelmstrasse shouting the 'Horst Wessel Lied' and other fighting songs.... Hitler looked down fondly from a window of the chancellery...so impressed that he turned and asked, 'How on Earth did [Goebbels] conjure up all these thousands of torches in the space of a few hours?'"

Now associated with Nazis, torchlight parades lost any popularity that they had left in the United States. Today, the only remnants of torchlight parades are candlelight vigils for causes such as AIDS or in memory of someone famous who has died, and perhaps—though this stretches the point—the upraised cigarette lighters at rock concerts.

The Tammany Tiger, symbol of the organization's ruthlessness and hunger for power, by cartoonist Thomas Nast.

Tammany Hall

Graft. Theft. Selling political offices. These are the spoils of political war, and no one collected them like New York's Tammany Hall. Founded in 1789 and operating for almost two centuries, Tammany was the richest, most powerful machine in American politics.

"The Tammany Society, which originated the whole show, was founded during the years immediately following the American Revolution as a benevolent and patriotic fellowship ostensibly dedicated to the memory of an ancient and venerable American Indian chief named Tammany," says historian Oliver E. Allen's *The Tiger: The Rise and Fall of Tammany Hall*. Its meeting place, Tammany Hall, became the name of the group's political wing.

A strong wing it was. During the 1850s and 1860s, reports Allen, Tammany chief William "Boss" Tweed stole from New York City's coffers as much as $200 million—a figure "worth at least ten times [as much] today." Tweed was "unquestionably the most powerful man in the city and state, if not the nation."

Boss Richard Croker, who held power from 1886 to 1902, not only ruled the city, he made sure that the city knew it. At one event, Allen notes, "When Croker made his ceremonial entrance, the band struck up 'Hail to the Chief'"—the fanfare usually reserved for the president of the United States.

Boss Charles Murphy guided politician Al Smith, the Democrats' presidential nominee in 1928. When Murphy died, "an estimated 50,000 persons lined nearby streets to pay their respects," says Allen.

Boss Carmine De Sapio sold judgeships and, says the *New York Times'* Jonathan Hicks, "could make—and break—[city] council members, mayors, and even governors."

De Sapio's reign in the 1950s was the last flash of Tammany power. Mayor Robert Wagner, whom De Sapio had helped to elect in 1953, turned against him in 1961. In 1963, De Sapio ran for Tammany district leader and lost. In the early 1970s, he was imprisoned for conspiring to bribe a city commissioner.

"He was undone by the reform movement within the Democratic Party," writes Hicks. In *Going, Going, Gone: Vanishing Americana*, authors Susan Jonas and Marilyn Nissenson add, "The bosses were often undone by their racist attitudes; the machines that had accommodated successive waves of Irish, Italian, Jewish, and Slavic immigrants were less willing to work with Blacks and Hispanics." During John Lindsay's mayoralty (1966–1973), Tammany died.

Nonetheless, Tammany kept on influencing elections. "Even after it had finally been swept away," Allen notes, "people could not believe it was no longer there, and politicians continued to run against it, successfully."

Students for a Democratic Society

SDS. The initials sparked arguments for nearly a decade.

"Students for a Democratic Society started in 1960 as an offshoot of a long-standing socialist group, the League for Industrial Democracy," writes John Button in *The Radicalism Handbook: Radical Activists, Groups and Movements of the Twentieth Century.* SDS leader Tom Hayden put it less formally. "We thought all things were possible, and out of that came SDS."

In 1962, 47 SDS members assembled in Port Huron, Michigan, and wrote a manifesto. The Port Huron Statement described SDS as "looking uncomfortably to the world we inherit.... If we appear to seek the unattainable, then let it be known that we do so to avoid the unimaginable." The paper offered "a vision of a transformed America [that] hit campuses with the force of a revelation," wrote *U.S. News and World Report*'s William Chaze.

The group didn't stop there. Says Button, "SDS provided training and support for many white participants in the early civil-rights protests, numerous leaders of the Vietnam antiwar and antidraft movements...and many of the women involved in the ideas and early actions of the women's liberation movement."

SDS grew. "By its height in 1968, SDS had become...an influential national organization with 350 official chapters and 100,000 members," says Button. *Commentary* magazine's Scott McConnell adds, "The organization had become the largest radical group in America since the 1930s."

Radical, indeed. At SDS's 1969 convention, "the leadership of SDS had begun to speak in Marxist–Leninist tongues," former SDS member Todd Gitlin wrote in *The Nation*. In October of that year, the Weathermen, a left-wing terrorist group, began setting off bombs; SDS split between pro- and anti-Weather factions, and fell apart.

SDS's collapse made waves. Journalist Jo Durden-Smith wrote in *California* magazine, "[The entire] Movement of the politically active...did indeed break down and lose its coherence in 1969 with the breaking up of [SDS.]" Nevertheless, says Button, "[SDS members had] developed a range of tactics which were to become commonplace in the 1970s: teach-ins, direct actions, consensus decision-making, and small group organization."

Black Panthers demonstrating in front of the New York State Supreme Court.

Opinions about SDS vary wildly. McConnell called it "a movement that...managed, in a period of about six years, to recapitulate the entire moral history of Western socialism, from the utopians to Stalinism."

Former SDS leader Bob Ross recalls it differently. At a reunion in 1986, he said, "Somewhere between the ages of 18 and 25 is a mighty opportunity to speak truth to power."

The Black Panthers

Thousands called the Black Panthers heroes, while the FBI tried to destroy them.

In 1966, Huey Newton and Bobby Seale—students

at Merritt College in Oakland, California—founded the Black Panther Party for Self-Defense. (In 1967, the party dropped "for Self-Defense.") It started bookstores, medical clinics, schools, and community centers. It ran voter-registration drives and gave ghetto children free breakfasts.

But mostly, says author John Button's *The Radicalism Handbook: Radical Activists, Groups and Movements of the Twentieth Century*, "[the Panthers] saw the BPP's chief role as monitoring police activities in black communities." The party stockpiled guns and offered black communities protection from police. In 1967, says *Essence* magazine, "armed Panthers invade[d] the capitol in California to protest legislation limiting their right to bear arms."

The party amassed 40 chapters with 5,000 members, but it had troubles. In 1967, Newton was arrested for killing an Oakland policeman. (He was eventually acquitted.) The next year, a gun battle with Oakland cops killed teenage Panther Bobby Hutton, and an armed fight at UCLA killed Panthers Bunchy Carter and John Huggins. In 1969, the year that Chicago cops killed Panthers Fred Hampton and Mark Clark, Seale was tried for incitement to riot; Judge Julius Hoffman denied him access to his lawyer and had him gagged and chained until the trial ended.

FBI chief J. Edgar Hoover named the Panthers "the single greatest threat to the internal security of the United States" and told his men to destroy them. They pushed Panthers and other African-American groups to fight each other. "By the end of the decade," Button writes, "28 Panthers had been killed." The violence and arrests overwhelmed members into quitting. Internal dissension split what was left of the party.

In 1974, police charged Newton with another murder; he fled to Cuba. Panther leader Eldridge Cleaver, jumping bail after violating parole, went to Algeria. By 1975, the Black Panther Party was effectively dead.

Yet its echoes persisted. In 1983, a repatriated Cleaver tried to start a new Panther party. ("I don't put any stock in any efforts that he has," Seale scoffed.) In 1990, Milwaukee alderman Michael McGee formed the Black Panther Militia "and threatened the city with all-out guerrilla warfare against whites unless his demands for millions of dollars in economic development, health care, and emergency employment programs were met," said *L.A. Weekly* journalist Joe R. Hicks.

In 1996, a group called the New Black Panther Party warned that its members would attend a Dallas school board meeting armed and angry that whites ran the mostly minority schools.

But the original Panthers, the militants who rallied thousands, are gone.

INTERNATIONAL AFFAIRS
Devil's Island

Ile du Diable, the world's most notorious penal colony. But what was it really all about?

The island still sits in the Atlantic Ocean eight miles from the east coast of South America, a part of French Guiana's Iles du Salut (Isles of Salvation or Isles of Safety, depending on your translation). It's not big—about 15 square miles—and its low, rocky terrain, though challenging, is not the world's harshest.

First settled in the 1850s, the island became infamous when the French government changed it from a leper colony to a penitentiary for political prisoners. The first and best-known was army captain Alfred Dreyfus, sent to the island in 1895 on a false charge of treason.

The smallest of the three penal colonies on the Iles du Salut and the nine other prisons that French Guiana maintained on the mainland, Devil's Island got its name from its landscape and the murderously choppy waters surrounding it. It became known as the "dry guillotine."

Although more than 50,000 prisoners were sent to the Iles du Salut, only 2,000 left alive, fewer than 30 by escaping. The first to survive an escape, alleged murderer Henri Charriere, fled on a raft of dried coconuts. His story became the 1973 Steve McQueen movie *Papillon*.

Of the French Guianan prisons, Devil's Island may not have forced prisoners into the worst conditions. But its colorful name made it the most famous. "Horror stories de luxe have told of men working stark naked in the sizzling tropical jungle, of lust, greed, murder, homosexuality in prison cages crammed with killers, rapists, thieves," *Time* magazine reported in 1938.

For years, international pressure to close Devil's Island mounted. Some of the loudest calls came from the English and American press and various Latin American nations. "It is not difficult to understand [the Latin Americans'] resentment toward

France in choosing a Latin American colony for a dumping ground for criminals and outcasts," a report from the French parliament observed.

In July 1938, French premier Edouard Daladier decreed that his country would no longer send prisoners to the Iles du Salut. The thousands living on the islands would stay until their terms were up, unless they died in the meantime. Hundreds did die there even though they had served out their terms; during World War II, France was too busy to free prisoners from Devil's Island.

In the early 1950s, the last prisoner left Devil's Island. He refused to reveal his identity. The world's most legendary prison was officially closed.

The Berlin Wall

"General Secretary Gorbachev, if you seek peace, if you seek prosperity for the Soviet Union and Eastern Europe, if you seek liberalization: Come here to this gate! Mr. Gorbachev, open this gate! Mr. Gorbachev, tear down this wall!"

President Ronald Reagan said those words (by speech writer Peter Robinson) in June 1987, standing by one of the gates of the Berlin Wall. Two years later, the wall would indeed be torn down.

Since Germany was cut into the communist East and capitalist West after World War II, 200,000 people had fled from East Berlin to freedom in West Berlin. On August, 13, 1961, the governments of the Soviet Union and East Germany erected the wall to stop the flow.

No handball playing here, pal—The Berlin Wall.

East German official Erich Honecker designed the Berlin Wall, and he did an effective job. The wall stretched over more than 26 miles of concrete and barbed wire. Armed guards, aided by floodlights, watched for anyone who might try to cross over without authorization. "The wall was the scene of the shooting of many East Germans who tried to escape," notes *Larousse Dictionary of World History*.

Western governments protested the construction of the wall. President John F. Kennedy visited the wall's western side to announce *"Ich bin ein Berliner"*—I am a Berliner, a declaration of solidarity with those trying to escape. But nothing short of war seemed likely to pull the wall down, and no president wanted a war with the Russians. The wall stayed in place for nearly 30 years.

In 1989, East Germany's leader was the wall's designer, Erich Honecker. But the

Soviet leader was Mikhail Gorbachev, who was liberalizing his country. Liberty proved contagious. In October, under pressure from his citizens and their desire for freedom, Honecker resigned. Three weeks later, says the history *Our Glorious Century*, "the new East German government held a press conference. Among the topics was a notice that all border restriction on crossing into West Germany would be lifted, effective that night."

East Germans by the thousand began passing through the wall, and East German troops began dismantling it. Ordinary citizens got into the show, wielding pickaxes and bare hands to rip the wall apart. Around the world, fascinated television viewers stared at their sets, watching a symbol of tyranny get literally ripped to pieces.

By the end of 1990—the year when Germany officially reunified—the entire wall was gone. The dream of presidents Kennedy and Reagan had come true.

The Soviet Union

A Soviet Parade in Red Square, 1969.

It was the Big Red Bear, the Beast in the East. One of its leaders promised to bury the United States; another was so ruthless that he annihilated millions of his own people.

During the Cold War, no one would have predicted that the Union of Soviet Socialist Republics would go quietly. The Soviet Union was, after all, the nation that put satellites into space before the U.S. government thought of it; the country that withstood Hitler's most savage assaults, lost 20 million people, and never gave up; the government that broke treaties and frustrated opponents but evaded attack. The USSR had problems, of course—it was an elephantine, expensive chore to govern—but every nation had problems, and the Soviets had been handling their bulky empire for decades. Few experts expected it to fall.

Nonetheless, it collapsed of its own weight, its lagging economy unable to pay for a defense establishment bloated and top-heavy from competing with American defense.

Even under the circumstances, the Soviet Union might still be around if consecutive Soviet leaders Leonid Brezhnev, Yuri Andropov, and Konstanin Chernenko hadn't died within three years, leaving the reform-minded Mikhail Gorbachev in charge. But even Gorbachev didn't predict that once the Russian people tasted his *glasnost* (openness) and *perestroika* (restructuring), they would want more and more until they insisted on freedom, elections, and capitalism.

More than one expert predicted that the Soviet leaders would panic, tighten their grip, and pound the people into silence. They didn't. They actually let go. Latvia, Lithuania, Estonia: You're free. Foreign investors: The walls barring you are down, come on in. Dissidents: We're opening the prison-camp gates. Stalingrad: You're St. Petersburg again. Cuba: You're on your own.

With the chaos and corruption that a newborn capitalist economy can bring, many Russians may yearn for the old days when the people in charge kept control. And some in the West may miss the days when the enemy was hard to miss and easy to define. But for most people, it is hard to have nostalgia for a regime that persecuted its own citizens, sponsored despots and wars around the globe, and contributed to making life miserable for half the planet.

Rest in peace, Soviet Union. Don't come back.

Apartheid

The word means "apartness," but it really meant racism, murder, imprisonment, and injustice. It was South Africa's official government policy for almost 50 years.

Even before apartheid became official policy, Blacks had no voice in Parliament, suffered harsh segregation, and faced restrictions in the job market. But apartheid made racism a comprehensive, nationwide system.

"The ideology had several roots," explains *The Cambridge Encyclopedia*. "Boer [white South African] concepts of racial, cultural, and religious separation arising out of their sense of national uniqueness; British liberal notions of indirect rule [allowing the Boers to run South Africa their own way]...and the concern for job protection, promoted by white workers to maintain their status."

Whites voted apartheid into power in 1948, when the pro-apartheid National Party won the country's elections. According to the *Dictionary of 20th Century History* by David Brownstone and Irene Franck, laws such as the Prohibition of Mixed Marriages Act (1949), Population Registration Act (1949–50), Immorality Act and Group Areas Act (both 1950), Prevention of Illegal Squatting Act (1951), and Bantu Authorities Act and Bantu Education Act (both 1953) established "punitive provisions aimed at Blacks, other non-whites and all opponents of the regime, including internal deportations and exiles, educational segregation, prohibition of interracial marriages and sexual activities, abolition of the right of Blacks to strike and the creation of Black 'homelands.'"

Humanitarian groups protested. In 1952, the United Nations issued the first of its several condemnations. The African National Congress, an antiracist South African citizens' organization, used civil disobedience and other methods; an ANC offshoot, the Pan-Africanist Congress, fought back as well.

Signs of apartheid.

But apartheid stayed. In fact, its chief architect, Hendrick Verwoerd, was prime minister on March 21, 1960, when in the Sharpeville township, "the police opened fire on a crowd demonstrating against [apartheid]…killing 69 people and wounding 180 others," reports the *Larousse Dictionary of World History*. The government banned the ANC and PAC, and in 1962 imprisoned ANC leader Nelson Mandela.

If government officials thought that those tactics would suppress the conflicts over apartheid, they were wrong. The conflicts—and the killings—got worse. Boycotts of South African trade spread worldwide.

Finally, in April 1994, South Africa held all-race elections. The elections killed apartheid and elected a new president: former prisoner Nelson Mandela.

all gone

Chapter Nine
MARKETING

To sell products, businesses will try anything. And they have.

The California Raisin Board commissioned claymation master Will Vinton to create commercials that would promote the wrinkly little grapes. Vinton created a national phenomenon. The four little fruits—Red, A.C., Beebop, and Stretch—sang and danced (to "I Heard it Through the Grapevine," naturally); they had an animated special on CBS (*Meet the Raisins*) in 1988 and a Saturday-morning series in 1989 and 1990; they even appeared with a Claymation-animated Michael Jackson.

In the 1950s and '60s, gasoline stations were attracting customers by giving away all sorts of premiums. Drinking glasses were among the most common, but there was a considerable variety, such as win-a-car and win-a-check gimmicks. "In 1955, the industry had spent $42 million on driveway premiums, but by the late 1960s, it was spending $150 million on trading stamps alone," say John Jakle and Keith Sculle, authors of *The Gas Station in America*. By the time of the gasoline shortages of the 1970s, though, gas was in such demand that the expensive premiums and gimmicks were no longer necessary.

Spuds McKenzie, ready to party.

It's hard to believe today, when the government has tightly restricted tobacco advertising, but at one time cigarettes were advertised constantly on TV. The dancing packs of Old Gold cigarettes in the early 1950s were among the first of several thousand ads and promos. "You can take Salem out of

WHEN SMOKERS **CHANGED** TO PHILIP MORRIS, *EVERY CASE OF IRRITATION OF NOSE OR THROAT – DUE TO SMOKING – EITHER CLEARED UP COMPLETELY, OR DEFINITELY IMPROVED!*

Facts reported in medical journals on clinical tests made by distinguished doctors . . . *Proving this finer cigarette is less irritant!*

Finer flavor...
less irritant...
America's
FINEST
Cigarette!

Johnny on the job.

the country, but you can't take the country out of Salem"; "Winston tastes good, like a cigarette should"; "a silly millimeter longer" (for Benson & Hedges' 101-millimeter cigarette)—these and other slogans and songs were instantly familiar to almost anyone growing up in the 1960s. By 1969, however, public pressure was pushing cigarette ads off the home screen.

More recently, Anheuser-Busch scored success with Spuds McKenzie, the Bud Light beer dog. Outfitted with a conical party hat or other festive gear, and surrounded by bikini models, the dog (and the catchphrase "Go, Spuds, Go!") was a staple in half-time commercials for years.

There have been endless other ads, promotions, retail venues, and other ways to remove money from wallets. A few of them follow.

ADVERTISING
"Call for Philip Morris"

His name was Johnny, and boy, was he cute. He had the face of a spunky cherub and a piercing B-flat tenor that called out one of America's best-known advertising slogans.

In 1847, tobacconist Philip Morris opened a shop in London. It was the birth of an empire. By the 1930s, the Philip Morris cigarette company had moved to New York and launched the Marlboro, Parliament, and Benson & Hedges brands. In 1933, it started a new brand, called Philip Morris.

A lot of other cigarettes were on the market, though. With the Depression on full, too many brands were chasing too few dollars for Philip Morris to make much money.

To put the brand over, PM advertising manager Milton Biow hit on an inspiration: a pageboy. "Pageboys seemed to suggest hotels and resorts that attracted wealthy guests—of the sort who could afford a 15-cent brand even in hard times," says Richard Kluger, author of *Ashes to Ashes: America's Hundred-Year Cigarette War, the Public Health, and the Unabashed Triumph of Philip Morris.*

"Now, Biow thought, with the arrival of electronic broadcasting…Biow's inquiries for a page with an unusual voice brought him to the lobby where little Johnny Roventini worked."

Johnny was little indeed. He was 22 but looked 13, thanks to a mysterious childhood ailment. In April, Johnny was on the job as a pageboy in Manhattan's New Yorker Hotel. "Biow gave the page 50 cents and asked him to announce a message for Philip Morris," says Kluger, "and Johnny scurried all over…emitting a vibrant, even piercing but never shrill cry: 'Call-l-l-l for-r-r-r Philip Maw-reeeees!'"

Biow loved it. He sped Johnny to NBC's radio studio. Philip Morris sponsored a weekly variety show on the network; on April 17, the new yell went over the air.

"Johnny's high-pitched 'Call for Philip Morris!' became one of the most familiar sounds on radio," says historian Susan Wagner in *Cigarette Country: Tobacco in American History and Politics*. "By 1940, the brand had won 7% of the national cigarette market."

Biow dressed Johnny in a pillbox hat, red jacket with gold buttons, and black pants with a red stripe, a costume inspired by an old *Philip Morris* magazine ad. "With his full, ruddy cheeks, which seemed androgynously rouged, he was adorable," says Kluger. "Before long, 100,000 life-size cardboard-cutout likenesses of the uniformed Johnny and foot-high statuettes of him were on their way to cigarette vendors all over the country for display purposes."

Eventually, the "Call for Philip Morris" campaign receded. The company withdrew Johnny and promoted another brand's symbol, who became even more famous than the little pageboy: the Marlboro Man.

Burma-Shave signs

From this in the 1920s:

Holler

Half a pound for

Half a dollar

Oh boy!

Shaving joy

Complexion save

Burma-Shave

To this in the 1960s:

Our fortune

Is your

Shaven face

It's our best

Advertising space

Burma-Shave

These were the rhymes on the Burma-Shave signs, which stood on roadsides all over America. At one line per sign, they caught the eye of drivers and sold a lot of shaving cream.

Burma-Shave came from Minneapolis' Odell family, and the signs from salesman Allan Odell. In *The Verse by the Side of the Road: The Story of the Burma-Shave Signs and Jingles* by Frank Rowsome Jr., Allan's brother Leonard says that Allan came up with the idea after seeing "a set of small serial signs advertising a gas station: Gas, Oil, Restrooms, things like that—maybe a dozen of them—and then at the end a sign would point into the gas station."

Allan's father, who ran the company, objected. Allan persisted. Says Leonard, Dad gave in "more to shut him up than anything else."

The first signs, written in 1925, didn't rhyme. "Shave the modern way/No brush/No lather/No rub-in/Big tube 35¢ drug stores/Burma-Shave" was a typical example. But by 1929, with "Every shaver/Now can snore/Six more minutes/Than before/By using/Burma-Shave," Burma-Shave found the rhymed format that it kept, with some variations, for more than 30 years.

"By 1938," reports the Berkeley Pop Culture Project's *The Whole Pop Catalog*, "there were more than 40,000 Burma-Shave signs on the nation's highways." Eventually, there were about 600 poems. A jingle-writing contest brought in 50,000 entries. Burma-Shave boasted six million customers.

The rise of freeways in the 1950s, allowing drivers to zip by too fast to read signs, diminished the rhymes' readership. Competition from radio, television, and print advertising, along with the rising costs of the signs themselves, made the roadside ads less effective and costlier. The Odells sold the company to Philip Morris, Inc., in 1963—the last year in which Burma-Shave planted new signs.

For years, people claimed to see the old signs still standing, their white lettering beaming out from the familiar red background: "If our road signs/Catch your eye/Smile/But don't forget to buy/Burma-Shave."

L.S./M.F.T.

Rarely does an advertising campaign become so famous that its slogan doesn't have to be spelled out, but that's what happened with L.S./M.F.T. The five initials and their odd slash mark were part of one of the pioneer advertising campaigns of this century.

George Washington Hill was behind it. In Frederik Pohl and C.M. Kornbluth's science-fiction novel *The Space Merchants*, advertising agencies run the world, and the adman protagonist calls Hill "the father of our profession." The ruthless, hard-driving Hill became president of American Tobacco, the parent company of Lucky Strike cigarettes.

Lucky Strikes were pretty old; the brand name dated back to 1871. Starting in 1917, Hill launched a blitz to bump up its sales. His first slogan, "It's toasted," made cancer-sticks seem as wholesome and welcome as a hot breakfast. "Within 18 months, the sales of Lucky Strikes were nearly six billion a year," says James Playsted Wood, author of *The Story of Advertising*.

Hill and advertising executive Albert Lasker followed up with an appeal to women, "Reach for a Lucky instead of a sweet"; the cheerful "Be happy, go Lucky"; and a subtly sexy phrase that inspired endless jokes, "So round, so firm, so fully packed."

The most famous slogan of all was "Lucky Strike means fine tobacco"— L.S./M.F.T. The company broadcast the words constantly on radio; it also put them in bold red letters on magazine ads featuring shrewd farmers examining tobacco leaves as if to declare them, yes, fine tobacco.

It worked. "As late as 1955, Lucky Strike led the field [of cigarette brands]," say Charles Goodrum and Helen Dalrymple in *Advertising in America: The First 200 Years*. The campaign kept going for many years.

More recently, though, Lucky Strike left the "fine tobacco" approach behind and concentrated on sex. "A 1986 Lucky Strike campaign featured beautiful, young models with lots of flesh showing and faces sullen, steamy, and rebellious," says Larry White, author of *Merchants of Death: The American Tobacco Industry*. "The slogan was 'Light My Lucky.'" More recently, the company has shown its models in more casual attitudes but with faces and bodies just as gorgeous as ever. The connection is unmistakable: smoke Luckies, and you'll get to hang around with people this cool.

George Washington Hill would be proud.

Mr. ZIP

He looks ridiculous: a little man with a mailbag hanging from somewhere near his chin, with a head as long as his torso and a boomerang for a right hand. But his bold, childlike design, big-eyed smile, and eagerness to give you your mail have made little Mr. ZIP endearing.

The Postal Service didn't create Mr. ZIP, or even commission him into existence. New York's Chase Manhattan Bank did.

Chase asked its advertising agency, Cunningham and Walsh, to create a campaign for its bank-by-mail system. C&W's Harold Wilcox, whose father was a mail carrier, designed the little man. According to the Postal Service, the character looked much as he does now, but he didn't have his mailbag. He was used a few times and then dropped.

The man himself.

Years passed. American Telephone and Telegraph (AT&T) company bought Cunningham and Walsh. And in 1962, the post office was in trouble. There was simply too much mail to sort and deliver promptly. To make the process easier, the post office invented ZIP codes, "ZIP" standing for Zoning Improvement Plan. But it wasn't enough.

According to *What A Character!: 20th Century American Advertising Icons*, by Warren Dotz and Jim Morton: "While on an airplane trip, [Postmaster General J. Edward Day] was fortunate enough to sit next to AT&T chairman Frederick Kappel. Kappel related the problems that the phone company encountered when it switched to digital dialing and area codes.... He warned Day that unless properly handled, the American public would reject postal zones." Indeed, a lot of Americans resented the idea that the post office could turn them into a set of numbers.

Kappel gave Day more than advice; he gave him, free of charge, the little mailman, who had been sitting idle in AT&T's files. Post office artists sharpened the mailman's limbs and torso, and gave him his mailbag.

At a convention of postmasters in October 1962, Mr. ZIP was unveiled. "Most trademarks need many years to gain public recognition," the Postal Service's "Origin of Mr. ZIP" write-up says, "but the Postal Service discovered that within four years of his appearance, 80% of the population knew who Mr. ZIP was and what he stood for."

Mr. ZIP passed into semiretirement when the Postal Service introduced the nine-digit ZIP + 4 code in 1983. He remained on the edges of some stamp sheets until 1986, when the Postal Service discontinued him permanently.

No doubt he's enjoying his rest. Neither rain nor snow nor sleet nor gloom of night can wipe that U-shaped grin off of his famous, flat face.

Joe Camel

Whether blowing sax in his blues band or nightclubbing in a tux, Joe Camel was all bad-boy suavity, with a cigarette always near.

Joe Camel was, in a sense, Joe II, son of the stately beast on the Camel cigarette pack, who was named Old Joe. British illustrator Nicholas Price designed young Joe in 1974 for French advertising; the hip dromedary moved into other countries as well.

He came to America in 1988, in time for Camel's 75th anniversary. The brand needed him. Sales were plummeting, and rival tobacco firm Philip Morris was trying to buy Camel's parent company, R.J. Reynolds.

Originally appearing under the slogan "75 years and still smokin'," Joe was soon known simply as Camel's "smooth character." He stopped the sales decline and helped RJR stay strong enough to push Philip Morris away.

But he overdid it. "His expression and outsize schnoz became fixtures not only on billboards but also on T-shirts, jackets, and other items coveted by youths," wrote the *Los Angeles Times'* Myron Levin. "In a 1991 study published by the *Journal of the American Medical Association*, Joe finished in a tie with Mickey Mouse among symbols most often recognized by children three to six years old."

It got worse. "In 1986, [Camel's] market share among underage smokers was less than 3%," noted a *Christian Science Monitor* editorial. "By 1993, [its] youth market share had grown to 13%." Janet Mangini, an attorney suing RJR over Joe, charged in the *Wall Street Journal*, "Sales of Camels to teenagers rose from $6 million in 1988, when the [Joe Camel] campaign started, to $476 million in 1992."

Joe became a target. "Anti-smoking activists convinced President Clinton, the

American Medical Association, several Surgeons General, the Federal Trade Commission, and other authorities that Joe Camel was…intended to appeal specifically to children to take up smoking," the *New York Times'* Stuart Elliott wrote.

By 1997, Joe was on the ropes. His ads appeared only in America. Even there, antismokers sued RJR to kill him. In May, the Federal Trade Commission sued, claiming that Joe encouraged kids to smoke. Attorneys general in 39 states sued, charging that smoking cost the states millions in Medicare and other costs.

On July 10, RJR spokesman Richard Williams announced that the company's ads would from then on show no Joe. While crediting the new campaign to simple marketing strategy, Williams admitted, "The controversy that swirled around Joe Camel was part of the reason we began looking at alternative campaigns in the first place."

Antismokers cheered. Bruce Reed, President Clinton's top domestic policy adviser, put it best. Said Reed, "Joe Camel is dead. He had it coming."

BRANDS AND PACKAGES
Cracker barrels

You could get almost anything at the old general store. You still can: Most neighborhood grocers carry fruit, coffee, kitty litter, batteries, cough syrup, newspapers, and all sorts of other things. There's at least one major difference, though: no cracker barrels.

The cracker barrel was an icon of rural life. With the lid on, it was a makeshift table for conversation or checkers. People who hung around the general store and gabbed about whatever hit their minds became known as "cracker-barrel philosophers."

It wasn't only crackers that came in barrels. There were "barrels of flour, barrels of red McIntoshes, barrels of 'West Indy' molasses…[and] barrels of potatoes from back-hill farms; of pickles, salt pork, sugar, and coarse salt," writes R.J. McGinnis in his book *The Good Old Days: An Invitation to Memory.* But crackers were perhaps the most common.

By the 1930s, the cracker barrel was on the wane. Mass-marketers of crackers and chips such as Nabisco were distributing their products in easy-to-carry boxes. No longer did customers have to scoop out crackers; they need only pick up a carton and be on their way. Moreover, the small, sealed boxes seemed to guarantee fresher merchandise than did big, open barrels that had been housing crackers for heaven knew how long.

Denied a place in reality, the cracker barrel became a legend. The movie *A Face in the Crowd* (1957) features a hillbilly entertainer, Lonesome Rhodes (Andy Griffith), who creates and stars in a TV show featuring "a bunch of country-looking characters" (as he contemptuously calls them) in a country store. Rhodes uses the show to sound off on politics and get his pet politician elected president. The show's title: *Lonesome Rhodes' Cracker Barrel.*

In 1992, *Forbes* magazine writer Toddi Gutner reported on Cracker Barrel Old Country Stores, a chain of "country-style, down-home restaurant–gift shops." Cracker Barrel recreates the symbols of authentic country stores and inns, from food (breakfast pancakes with real butter and maple syrup, catfish for dinner) to decor (wood-beamed ceilings, pot-bellied stoves) to merchandise (woodcrafts and preserves). Starting with one store in Lebanon, Tennessee, founded in 1969, the chain reached more than 100 by the 1990s, primarily in the Southeast.

So the cracker barrel, apparently outmoded and obsolete, remains strong as a marketing tool. It makes sense, actually—the cracker barrel existed to help sell products—and if that's not a marketing tool, what is?

Esso, Humble, Enco, Enjay, and Jersey Standard gasoline

"Put a tiger in your tank!"

That was the motto of Esso gas, whose cartoon tiger was one of the 1960s' most familiar icons. But after years of work and more than $100 million, Esso disappeared.

In 1911, Standard Oil dominated 75 percent of America's petroleum industry. The Supreme Court convicted Standard of restraint of trade and chopped it into 34 disparate firms. Among them was Standard Oil of New Jersey. The company created Esso (for S.O.) and took the brand national in 1926.

Other Standard Oils (California, Indiana, and Ohio had their own Standards) sued, claiming that customers would confuse Esso with them. The courts ruled that Standard of New Jersey could market Esso in only 18 states and the District of Columbia. So the company used Enco (for Energy Company) in non-Esso states—except Ohio, whose Standard Oil company declared that Enco was too close to Esso; Standard of New Jersey used the name Humble there. It named other divisions Jersey Standard and Enjay (for N.J.).

Your friendly Esso station.

The result, said *Time* magazine, was "decades of grappling with the national advertising and marketing problems that a multiplicity of trademarks entails."

In the 1960s, Standard of New Jersey began seeking one name for all of its divisions. The *Wall Street Journal*'s James Tanner wrote, "[Researchers] spent three years poring over dictionaries and using computers, committees, and investigators." They scoured 55 languages for a word "that seemed to stick in consumers' minds and had no obscene or embarrassing meanings in any foreign tongue," said *Time*. In a breakthrough, researchers found that they could deploy a double X, as only Maltese used that combination.

They chose Exxon. On June 21, 1972, Standard of New Jersey declared Humble, Jersey Standard, Enco, Enjay, and Esso things of the past (though Esso did hang on in Europe).

Signs changed at 25,000 service stations. Among other things that needed replacing, Tanner said, were "300 million sales slips and other service-station forms...[plus] plaques for 22,000 oil wells, and the names on 18,000 other buildings and storage tanks."

More trouble arose. "Stockholders complained that the new name sounds like a 'laxative,' a 'detergent,' or a 'medicine,'" wrote *New York Times* reporter William Smith. Artist Robert Aries claimed that he'd already trademarked the Exxon name. Nebraska governor J.J. Exon, who owned an office-supply house named Exon's Inc., fought Exxon, got a settlement, changed his firm's name to J.J. Exon Co., and let the oil company register Exxon as its own.

Large though these headaches were, they were soon over. Esso was gone. The company no longer encouraged drivers to put a tiger in their tanks.

Compact disc longboxes

Billy Joel probably didn't know that he was starting a revolution, but he was. In 1982, the singer's 1978 *52nd Street* was the first album sold as a compact disc.

A flood of CDs followed. Record stores switched from the old LP in its 12-by-12-inch cover to the CD's 12-by-6 cardboard "longbox" (as the record industry named the package). The box was small enough to fit two in one LP rack but bulky enough to hinder theft—a grave concern, since the CD's small size made it easy to steal.

Since a plastic case (a "jewel box") inside the longbox protected the CD, many buyers threw the box out. The waste angered the ecologically minded, including rockers Don Henley, Peter Gabriel, Sting, and the members of U2.

Anti-box forces noted that only the United States used the longbox and that foreign retailers had few problems using only the jewel box. They scoffed at retailer claims that thieves would steal jewel boxes, since retailers carried the even smaller cassette tapes with no hesitation. They added that record companies would save money by not having to pay for the boxes. In 1989, Robert Simonds, chief financial officer of the record company Rykodisc, founded the Ban the Box Coalition, a group of musicians, record companies, and record-industry associations.

To oppose Ban the Box, cardboard makers founded the Entertainment Packaging Association. Retailers, dreading the costs of re-racking, also wanted to keep the box.

In 1990, children's music star Raffi became the first act to release a CD sans longbox. Other musicians followed. The same year, state legislators in New York and California proposed outlawing the box. Congressman Al Swift, chairman of the House Subcommittee on Transportation and Hazardous Waste, planned a federal anti-box law.

In late February 1992, record executives went to New York for the Grammy Awards (one of the few times that they were in the same city). They used the opportunity to discuss the longbox situation.

Bob Dylan goes long, 1989.

The cover of the
first Sears catalog,
advertising "The
Cheapest Supply
House on Earth."

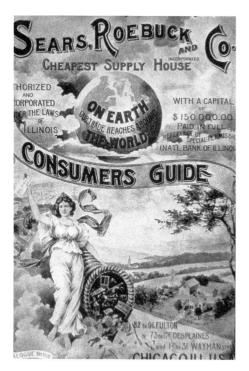

In March, they announced that the jewel box would be "the new standard package size for compact discs in the United States, beginning in April 1993," reported Paul Verna and Ed Christman in the record-industry trade journal *Billboard*. "The move seals the coffin of the infamous 6-by-12-inch cardboard long-box." Retailers didn't like it, but they adjusted. The coffin was indeed sealed.

RETAILING
Sears Catalog

For more than a century, it was the Wish Book.

It began in 1888, with a catalog sent out by watch salesman Richard Sears, offering watches and jewelry. The book was so successful that Sears put out a 753-page general merchandise catalog—including not just watches and jewelry but clothing, farm implements, and all other kinds of merchandise—in 1896.

For people living far from a big city's variety of stores, the twice-yearly catalog was a godsend. Author R.J. McGinnis writes in his book *The Good Old Days: An Invitation to Memory*, "Entire farms were equipped from the Sears catalog," which offered "machinery, saddles, harness, fence, building material, and home furnishings."

Moreover, McGinnis adds, "It was the only contact with the elegant life of the cities for millions of American farm dwellers." It was filled with sterling silver tableware, tailor-made suits of silk and velvet, and (in the words of the catalog) "solid gold Bohemian garnet and amber jewelry." From abdominal corsets and accordion flutes to zither tuning hammers and Zulu brand shotguns (at $3.40 apiece), the catalog and its 6,000-plus items were wondrous.

In 1927, Sears distributed 15 million catalogs throughout the United States. By 1940, the company was receiving three million requests for catalogs every year, according to *The Good Old Days: A History of American Morals and Manners as Seen Through the Sears Roebuck Catalogs* by David L. Cohn. New editions kept up with modern times (the 1990s' books offered entertainment centers, mastectomy bras, Sega game gear, and other current items), and then kept growing; the 1992 catalogs ran about 1,600 pages.

But bigness has its costs. On January 25, 1993, Sears announced that it would stop producing the Big Book by the end of the year and eliminate "about 3,400 full-time and 16,500 part-time positions" associated with the catalog.

Instead of the book that meant all things to many people, Sears planned to distribute "smaller specialty and promotional catalogs." There was one for power and hand tools, one for bed and bath accessories, one for "women's apparel in sizes 14 and larger," and eventually catalogs for auto supplies, NBA and NFL sports apparel, leather apparel, and other merchandise.

But the Big Book, thick as a fist and crammed with delights, became a relic of the past.

Gimbel's

"Does Macy's tell Gimbel's?" That rhetorical question popped up whenever anyone was asked if he shared secrets with a competitor. But today, Macy's can't tell Gimbel's anything. Gimbel's isn't there to hear.

Adam Gimbel, a Bavarian who came to the United States in 1835, wandered along the Mississippi river, selling notions out of a pack. Eventually, he settled in Vincennes, Indiana, a Wabash River frontier town. In 1842, the 27-year-old set up a trading post.

"Fairness and Equality of All Patrons, whether they be Residents of the City, Plainsmen, Traders, or Indians" was Gimbel's motto. In the 1870s, he expanded to a three-story emporium that he called the Palace of Trade. During 1887, he set up his first branch store, in Milwaukee.

Gimbel died in 1896, but his sons were running the business, and they reached for the big prize: New York. In 1909–1910 they established a store on Herald Square, a block from Macy's. A feud was on.

Gimbel's was aggressive. The company hired executives from Macy's, bought the Saks Company in 1923 (and opened Saks Fifth Avenue in '24), added other retail houses, and established stores under its own name in Miami, Chicago,

Gimbel's, New York City, 1920.

117

Detroit, San Francisco, and Beverly Hills. Eventually, there were 36 Gimbel's stores. The company's annual sales topped $800 million.

Sometimes, Gimbel's innovated. "Gimbel's was the first American department store to hold a public art auction (New York, 1941) and the first to sell furnished cooperative apartments displayed at the store (Philadelphia, 1953)," writes historian Robert Hendrickson in *The Grand Emporiums: The Illustrated History of America's Great Department Stores*.

Nonetheless, profits eventually dropped. In 1973, the company sold out to tobacco firm Brown and Williamson.

B&W didn't help Gimbel's. "In an era when major retailers have been under severe pressure from the so-called 'off-price' and discount stores," wrote *Newsweek*, "Gimbel's has failed to upgrade its image." Not that the company didn't try. "An attempt by Gimbel to tap the affluent market with its second Manhattan store, which opened in the early 1970s at 86th Street, has not borne fruit," the *New York Times'* Isadore Barmash reported.

In 1986, Brown and Williamson's parent company, B.A.T. Industries, gave up. Gimbel's held a final sale, cutting prices furiously, and then closed.

The Automat

Put in your money, take out some food. That simple concept fed Americans for almost 90 years.

Joseph Horn of Philadelphia, age 27, didn't like working for his family's surgical-implement business. He wanted to open a restaurant. He ran a newspaper ad and got Frank Hardart, age 38, new in town and experienced at restaurant work. The men became partners and in 1888 opened a lunch counter.

It didn't satisfy them. Hardart visited Europe to study its best restaurants. "On his return, he announced proudly that he had paid the Quisiana Automat Company of Berlin $30,000 for equipment similar to the apparatus installed in that city's famous 'waiterless' restaurant," write authors Susan Jonas and Marilyn Nissenson in the book *Going, Going, Gone: Vanishing Americana*.

Horn and Hardart opened the first American Automat in Philadelphia in 1902. It was instantly popular.

Like others who have successes at home, Horn and Hardart set eyes on New

York. In 1912, they opened the city's first Automat, near Times Square.

"Machinery with splendor," author John Mariani (*America Eats Out*) has called the Automat, "its ornate wooden framework sparkling with beveled, mirrored surfaces, its uppermost edges alternating between swelling arches." Jonas and Nissenson add, "The Automat had a stained-glass window 30 feet wide and two stories high, designed by Nicola D'Ascenzo, who also created windows for New York's Episcopal Cathedral of St. John the Divine. The moldings of the dining room were carved with leafy branches laden with apples and pears."

"On the first day," Jonas and Nissenson note, "the Automat took in 8,693 nickels." Horn and Hardart's empire grew to 60 take-out shops (with the famous motto "Less Work for Mother"), 160 Automat restaurants, and thousands of employees. Everyone ate at Automats, but "the core constituency was the lower middle class—office workers and others who wanted to eat cheaply," noted journalist Richard Papiernik in *Nation's Restaurant News.*

The times changed, but the Automats didn't. In the 1960s, fast-food chains such as McDonald's took the customers who wanted a tasty, cheap meal. On December 28, 1968, the first Automat closed.

By the 1990s, only one Automat was left, at the corner of 42nd Street and Third Avenue in Manhattan. On April 9, 1991, it closed.

But the habit of pulling food from slots remains. When you put money in a vending machine for a Mars bar, think of the Automat—and thank the farsighted Horn and Hardart.

Breakfast at the Automat, 1940.

all gone

PEOPLE AND PROFESSIONS

Whenever a new machine comes along to do a job—robots to make cars, for example—the humans who are already doing that job protest. As well they should, because automation, federal law, and just plain economic bad times do indeed wipe out jobs and entire professions.

Take the humble soda jerk. Always there with a smile, he dispensed malts, sundaes, and phosphates for anyone with enough pocket change. His name came from the early 1900s, when it apparently took a hard yank on a soda-fountain tap to get its fluid to flow. But as Susan Jonas and Marilyn Nissenson write in *Going, Going, Gone: Vanishing Americana*, "during World War II, soda jerks were drafted, sugar was rationed, and fountain equipment was not manufactured. Afterward, soda fountains never fully revived"—although modern retro diners do take a good try at it.

Another emblem of days past is the uniformed gas station attendant, who came to prominence when mere filling stations became full-service stations in the 1930s. When you drove over the station's long, black rubber bell, its signature "ding!" alerted a young man in a station outfit (with his name stitched on a round breast patch) to jump out wielding squeegee, chamois, and an offer to check your oil. Oil companies used the pump jockeys in advertisements: "You can trust your car to the man who wears the star—the big, bright Texaco star!" But starting in the 1960s, rising labor costs made attendants too expensive for many stations, vehicles needed less service, and self-service gas, cheaper than the full-service variety, became steadily more popular. You can still find a uniformed attendant at stations that have full-serve islands, but he's no longer an omnipresent part of the business.

Then there's the elevator operator, needed back when the first elevator for passengers was installed, in 1857, to bring the car to the passengers by turning a crank that raised and lowered it. Making the car land evenly was a specialized skill. Yet self-leveling elevators that came when you called them were eventually developed, with the first completely self-service elevator beginning operation in 1950. Today the few elevator operators that are still around exist only to dress up fancy buildings.

Some people pursue not just a career but a way of life, only to find that the next generation wants nothing to do with it. For instance, a startling number of light-skinned African Americans tried passing for White, keeping their true race secret until they died. But as Black pride spread and rose in the 1960s, passing for white became unnecessary and repugnant to any self-respecting Black man or woman.

And yet others look for truth, only to find it elusive. In the 1970s, teenage Guru Maharaj Ji and his Divine Light Mission attracted thousands of followers, but the movement receded when followers grew disenchanted with the Guru.

The old order passeth.

Civil War veterans

"When I was a boy, there were many Civil War veterans scattered around the community. They formed a tight little group which the stay-at-homes referred to, on the sly, as the Liars Club." So writes R.J. McGinnis in his book *The Good Old Days: An Invitation to Memory*. "[The veterans] got special consideration at family reunions and picnics, and on the Fourth of July and Memorial Day, they put on their old campaign caps and paraded behind the band."

Like other vets, Civil War veterans had an advantage during election years. In the book of essays *Enjoy, Enjoy!,* journalist Harry Golden writes, "For many years, the candidates with the best chance to win public office in the South were the men who had lost an arm or a leg in the Civil War." Golden says that a young lawyer, running against old vets whose campaign speeches consisted of retelling how they had fought in the war, had had enough. "Finally, the young lawyer took the rostrum. He said, 'I did not have the opportunity of fighting in the war. I am just a young lawyer, and I have both arms and both legs, but I want to assure you citizens that I have the biggest rupture in Anson County." Golden doesn't record whether or not the young lawyer won the election.

A remarkable number of Civil War veterans lived well into the 20th century, their war stories often getting more heroic with each year. Nearly 2,000 of them gathered at Gettysburg in 1938, 75 years after the battle on that site, to watch President Roosevelt dedicate the Eternal Light Peace Memorial.

The last Union soldier, former 17-year-old drummer boy Albert Woolrich, died in 1956 at (reportedly) age 109. The last Confederate, Walter Williams, lasted a little longer and died, allegedly at age 117, in 1959—98 years after the start of the Civil War.

Beatniks

Cool, baby: Beatniks Lenore Kandel and Marty Canter downing java and chatting it up, 1958.

"On October 13, 1955, nearly 100 people packed into the Six Gallery in San Francisco to hear six new poets read. Bottles of wine were passed. At about 11 that evening, the last reader, a horn-rimmed intellectual hepcat with wild black hair, stepped up to the front, and the crowd yelled, 'Go! Go! Go!' as he began chanting, his arms outstretched.... With his poem 'Howl,' Allen Ginsberg had just given voice to the Beat Generation." So wrote an anonymous journalist in *Sunset* magazine.

There have been more definitions of the Beat Generation than, most likely, there were beatniks. "Literary rebels who battled the alienation and conformity of the 1950s in their own jazz-inflected voice." "Modern-day nihilists for whom it was enough, apparently, to flout and deny." "The literary arm of the environmental movement." "The first movement to use the media to shape their own image, to mythologize themselves." "An avant-garde, anti-materialist group." "The consummate outsiders." "Stone-age hippies."

"Beat" meant thoroughly fatigued and worn down; it meant musical rhythm, especially the rhythms of jazz by such modern masters as Charlie Parker; and it meant beatification—or so Beat author Jack Kerouac (*On the Road*) and others claimed after the term became famous. No matter what its meaning, "Beat" involved experiences uncommon among suburban squares. The Beats were open-minded about sex and drugs, and disdained materialism, racial discrimination, and uniformed violence.

The first Beat was Herbert Huncke (rhymes with "junkie"). *New York Times* journalist Robert Thomas Jr. has described him as "the charismatic street hustler, petty thief, and perennial drug addict who enthralled and inspired a galaxy of acclaimed writers and gave the Beat Generation its name." These writers included Ginsberg, Kerouac, and William S. Burroughs (*Naked Lunch*).

Although Beats socialized with each other in San Francisco, New York, and other cities, they never formed a coherent movement as advocates of civil rights or women's liberation would. The leading Beats were poets and novelists, not orators evangelizing for converts.

After a few years, the Beats' fame dissipated. Kerouac died in 1978; Ginsberg and Huncke in 1996; Burroughs in 1997.

In recent years, young hipsters have imitated Beat style: poetry readings, a taste for drugs, and antiestablishment attitudes. The Beatniks are gone, but the Beat goes on.

Hippies and flower children

1965. Poet Allen Ginsberg coins the phrase "flower power." The Grateful Dead is formed. Harvard professor Timothy Leary recommends, "Turn on, tune in, drop out." San Francisco's Fillmore Auditorium begins presenting rock shows.

"City streets and college campuses were swarming with a new breed of alienated youth called hippies," says *Our Glorious Century*, from the Reader's Digest Association. "Hippies were a gentle lot.... They donned headbands, love beads, peace symbols, and flowers."

On January 14, 1967, in San Francisco's Golden Gate Park, 20,000 hippies convened their first big gathering: the Human Be-In. The Grateful Dead, Jefferson Airplane, and other bands played. Hippies shared food and drugs, and dispersed peacefully.

In June, the Monterey International Pop Festival drew 50,000 hippies to see Jimi Hendrix, Janis Joplin, and other acts, kicking off what hippies called the Summer of Love. Young people left Mom and Dad for crash pads, odd jobs, and dope.

America noticed. Gray Line Bus Tours presented a "Hippie Hop" through San Francisco's Haight-Ashbury district. Conservatives

A hippie and his hair.

ordered hippies to get a haircut and a job. Hippies responded, too: In October 1967, writes Robert Draper in *Rolling Stone Magazine: The Uncensored History*, "a casket was marched through Golden Gate Park and set aflame. 'The Death of the Hippie, devoted son of mass media,' [the marchers] proclaimed."

Soon, the hippies' life got hard. To their dismay, America elected the conservative Richard Nixon president in 1968. In 1969, Hell's Angels at a hippie-filled Rolling Stones concert beat several spectators and killed one. By 1970, Haight-Ashbury "looked like a plundered graveyard," writes Draper. *Our Glorious Century* adds, "Crime became rampant. The food supply dwindled, and growing numbers of sick, tired, hungry flower children began an exodus."

The exodus led many hippies to communes. Rural areas of Oregon, northern California, and New Mexico saw hippies living together, farming, and sharing their possessions. But personality conflicts, weak organization, poverty, and hatred from non-hippie neighbors killed many communes. Within a decade, the hippie movement was for the most part gone.

Yet as journalist Patty Campbell has written, "much of the hippie heritage was quietly absorbed into the mainstream and is still with us." The popularity of meditation, organic food, environmentalism, and the freedom to live one's own way rather than by tradition—all hallmarks of hippie life—remain vital.

Playboy Bunnies

Playboy magazine promotion director Victor Lownes started it. In 1959, says journalist Russell Miller's book *Bunny: The Real Story of Playboy*, the magazine printed a story on nightspots called Gaslight clubs, "which featured buxom cocktail waitresses laced into saucy costumes." Miller continues: "More than 3,000 readers wrote in to ask how they could join a Gaslight club. Lownes was astonished by the response and suggested to Hefner that they should think of doing something similar."

They did, working with nightclub manager Arnie Morton. Ilse Taurins, one of Lownes' girlfriends, "suggested dressing the waitresses like the Playboy rabbit logo," says Miller.

Hefner objected—his rabbit was male, after all—but Taurins returned the next day in "a kind of satin corset with a fluffy ball pinned to her backside and a curious pair of ears attached to her head," says Miller. Hefner and company added a bow tie, collar, and cuffs, and hiked up the corset's sides to show more leg. Voilà—the Bunny.

On February 29, 1960, in Chicago, the first *Playboy Club* opened, to huge success. More followed: Pittsburgh, Cincinnati, Baltimore, New York, St. Louis, Phoenix, Atlanta, Omaha, Boston, Detroit, Miami, Dallas, and elsewhere—22 in the United States alone, with more in London, Montreal, Paris, and other cities. Nearly a million customers paid $25 apiece for a "key" that gave them membership to the clubs, which were designed as lavish, sophisticated bachelor pads.

Bunnies on the job at a Playboy Club.

For the Bunnies, things were not so plush. In 1963, journalist Gloria Steinem went undercover as a Bunny. Her report was "an exposé of nasty and degrading job conditions, of stuffing the bosom of a too-tight, electric-blue-and-orange costume with athletic socks, of painful high heels, of a physical that included an internal exam, of heavy-breathing customers, of Bunnies who were supporting children, and most of all, of wages that averaged far less than the help-wanted ad stated," writer Marcia Cohen summarized in *The Sisterhood: The True Story of the Women Who Changed the World.*

Soon, the sexual revolution, women's liberation, and other developments made the Playboy Clubs old-fashioned—and worse, unprofitable. Playboy Enterprises closed several clubs and changed others—it even hired male Bunnies—but nothing helped.

On August 1, 1988, Playboy Bunnies were still at work, but only overseas. The previous day, the Lansing, Michigan, club—the last Playboy Club in America—had shut down.

Newsboys

A newsboy with a hot headline, eager to get that stack out of his hands.

"Extra! Extra! Read all about it! Lynching in Alabama!"

"Get it here! Mayor found in model's boudoir!"

"Paper, mister? Big panic on Wall Street today!"

Those were the calls of the newsboys, who peddled their papers on street corners nationwide. In 1933 alone, half a million were at work, according to the American Newspaper Publishers Association.

Newsboys go back as far as the mid-1800s. At first, they primarily delivered papers to subscribers, but soon they were celebrated for their entrepreneurial pluck in selling to anyone who passed by. Novelist Horatio Alger often made newsboys the heroes of his rags-to-riches sagas. "In 1895, a statue was erected in Great Barrington, Massachusetts, to honor newsboys," writes media historian and college professor Jon Bekken in the book *Newsworkers*.

Not that their life was easy. Rarely did they make more than $9.00 per week, and often less than $2.00. The average newsboy had to buy his papers from the publisher (and lost money if he couldn't sell them).

"Publishers entered into agreements with each other to prevent newsboys from playing them against each other to win better wages," Bekken reports. A publisher even might hire muscle—including gangster Lucky Luciano—to force newsboys into selling its paper alone, cutting them off from selling other papers. In the late 1800s, newsboys formed unions to fight back, with spotty, often short-lived success.

In 1938, the Fair Labor Standards Act outlawed child labor. After World War II, Americans spread to the suburbs, making it harder for a street-corner city kid to reach customers by yelling. Competition from television news triggered a slide in newspaper readership. The surviving publishers relied increasingly on the transparent-faced metal stand that opens when a customer drops in some change—the cheap, docile newspaper vending machine. By 1993, according to the Newspaper Association of America, newsboys sold less than 1 percent of all papers.

"Media historians have waxed eloquent on the roles of the publishers and editors who built the great newspapers and newspaper empires of the modern age," Bekken says. "They might do better to turn their attention to the newsboys, whose underpaid labor brought those newspapers to the public."

all gone

Chapter Eleven

PLACES AND STRUCTURES

Hotel Deauville and Traymore Hotel, Atlantic City.

Austin Building, Pullman Building, and Crane Mansion, Chicago.

Pruitt-Igoe housing projects, St. Louis.

Wayne Minor Houses, Kansas City.

Northwest Bank, Minneapolis.

Cosmopolitan Hotel, Denver.

King Cotton Hotel, Memphis.

Palomino Club, Los Angeles.

Hotel Dorset, New York.

Crystal Palace, London.

Mechanics Hall, Boston.

They're all gone now. The Cosmopolitan, Deauville, King Cotton, Pruitt-Igoe, Northwest, and Wayne Minor structures were blown up. The enormous glass and cast-iron Crystal Palace, a world-renowned exhibition hall turned amusement park, accidentally burned down. The Palomino, home to urban cowboys, simply went out of business after decades of presenting country and rock stars such as Jerry Lee Lewis and Emmylou Harris.

Nothing is more thoroughly "not there anymore" than a destroyed building. When they go, they take memories with them. For example:

Larkin Administration Building, Buffalo, New York. Built in 1903, it was arguably architect Frank Lloyd Wright's first masterpiece. "The five-story red brick building and its three-story annex were a monumental exercise in solid geometry, with spheres atop towering piers and blocklike corner stair towers," writes Carla Lind, author of *Lost Wright: Frank Lloyd Wright's Vanished Masterpieces*. "Fountains marked the entrance, and geometric patterns on oversized pier capitals drew the eye upward 76 feet to the top of the glass-roofed central court.... The acoustical plan was so successful that the central light court was amazingly quiet despite the more than 1,000 workers within the great space. The building included a rooftop terrace, conservatory, library, bakery, and restaurant." Unfortunately, years of poor management and neglect left the building in bad shape. The city of Buffalo took it over and destroyed it in 1950 to make room for a truck terminal.

Cincinnati's Coney Island. Yes, there was a Coney Island in Cincinnati. One of many amusement parks to come and go, expert Al Griffin, in his book *"Step Right Up, Folks!"*, called it "the best-managed amusement park in the entire country...operating the largest and most elaborate excursion steamer in the world." It had the usual amusement-park attractions, plus a wide, grassy mall. In the early part of the century, the park sold nickel rides on that new contraption, the automobile. But the Ohio River flooded it repeatedly, and the park closed in 1971, at age 86. Its legacy lives on, though. Coney Island was so clean that Walt Disney Productions asked the park's owner, Edward Schott, to help plan Disneyland.

Freedomland, New York. *Life* magazine called it "the latest, largest, and most elaborate" of late-1950s' funlands. "The massive park, built in the shape of the U.S. territorial outline, featured regional shows in appropriate geographical sections," explains Griffin. Shortly after the opening, though, a stagecoach accident injured 10 people, one of whom fractured her spine. "Plans for a TV show, like those that flocked for Disneyland, fell through," adds journalist Russell Miller. "The summer the park opened, armed robbers stole $28,836 from a business office." Even worse, Freedomland was dull. It closed in 1964.

Riverview Park, Chicago. What a place! "Riverview Park held the distinction of always presenting the newest and most exciting riding devices on its two-mile midway," says Gary Kyriazi, author of *The Great American Amusement Parks: A Pictorial History*. "One of its six roller coasters, the 'Bobs,' was...the fastest roller coaster in the nation. It was finally topped in sales in 1959 by the park's newest roller coaster, the 'Fireball,' which dropped down 90 feet to a pile of rocks, ducking underneath them at the last second." In the park's Parachute Jump, "passengers were slowly lifted up a tower 220 feet high, from where they were dropped in a stomach-lunging descent. About 80 feet from the top, the parachute would billow out, slowing the descent and gently lowering the terrified couple to the ground." Gangs and racial clashes soured this playland. Opened in 1906, Riverview closed in 1969.

Hacienda Hotel, Las Vegas. Unlike other Vegas hotels, the Hacienda was always "relaxed and unpretentious," says Bob Sehlinger, author of *The Unofficial Guide to Las Vegas*. Its entertainment, buffet, and swimming pool were of exceptionally high quality, but that apparently wasn't enough. In the flashiest event of its career, the hotel was blown up "on New Year's Eve [1996] before an audience of half a million delirious tourists and millions of television viewers across the country," wrote journalist David Samuels in *Harper's*.

These stories are typical of the great buildings and structures. And speaking of buildings and structures, let's enter some in depth.

Luna Park at night, around 1910.

AMUSEMENT PARKS
Luna Park

"Electric Eden." "A fairyland almost beyond belief." "An enchanted storybook land." For 43 years, Luna Park on New York's Coney Island inspired these and other praises.

Luna had rides. The Mountain Torrent shot passengers down, around, and through a mountain "in a flume carrying water at 35,000 gallons a minute, ending in a splash," writes Gary Kyriazi, author of *The Great American Amusement Parks*. The Tickler, a tub on wheels, spun its victims in all directions as it whirled along a corkscrew maze. In Witching Waves, "a flexible metal floor...moved up and down in wavelike motions as riders tried to steer their two-passenger cars," journalist Al Griffin writes in *"Step Right Up, Folks!"*

Luna had shows. In War of the Worlds, foreign navies zeroed in on New York until U.S. ships sank them. Fire and Flames offered "the actual burning of a four-story building, complete with firemen and a rescue squad to save actual men and women trapped in the upper stories," says Kyriazi. In Trip to the Moon, he adds, "Projections against the walls and floor gave the illusion of a blastoff.... The ship itself swayed and gave a feeling of motion.... The spaceship would approach the moon and cruise over its prairies, canyons, and craters before making a landing. The passengers would then debark...at a grotto where the Man in the Moon sat on a throne, surrounded by dancing moon maidens."

Luna's most stunning feature was itself. In *Coney Island: A Postcard Journey to the City of Fire*, historian Richard Snow reports, "Luna's every bulge and spike was defined by strings of light bulbs." As night fell, wrote author Albert Bigelow Paine, "Towers that had grown dim suddenly broke forth in electric outlines." *Scientific American* added, "Enough light is being used to illuminate a city of 500,000."

Luna was born from the 1901 Pan-American Exposition in Buffalo, New York, which included a moon voyage. George Tilyou, owner of the Coney Island amusement park Steeplechase Park, hired the ride's creators, Frederic Thompson and Elmer Dundy, to bring it to Steeplechase. It was a success. With the profits, Thompson and Dundy bought another Coney attraction, Sea Lion Park. On its site they built Luna, naming it not for the moon ride but for Luna Dundy, Elmer's sister.

On Luna's opening day in May 1903, 43,000 people crowded its 22 acres. An immediate success, the park earned back its million-dollar cost in three months.

Luna was a hit so big that its owners may have taken it for granted. Griffin writes, "Season after season, Luna Park was operated without adding any new attractions, and existing ones were run without proper maintenance until they simply fell apart. Patronage petered out accordingly."

In 1946, a fire destroyed Luna Park. Those who loved the old funland considered the flames a sort of euthanasia.

Glen Echo Park

A place full of dizzying silliness near Washington, D.C., may seem redundant. Still, Glen Echo Park provided more than 15 acres of fun to the area's residents—until racism and violence brought it down.

In the late 1800s, brothers Edward and Edwin Baltzley, rich from creating a splatterless eggbeater, went into real estate. In a Maryland forest, they built the Glen Echo Cafe, "a rambling series of dining halls, alcoves, and bridges," writes the *Christian Science Monitor*'s Amy Kaslow. It burned down. The Baltzleys then built houses and an 8,000-seat amphitheater for the Chautauqua Assembly, a church-sponsored education program. In the late 1880s, rumors of malaria chased patrons away.

Again Glen Echo changed tone, becoming an amusement park. In 1911, the Washington Railway and Electric Company trolley company bought it. A WREC line ended there; to put riders on its trolleys, WREC made Glen Echo a high-profile attraction.

"There is the Dodgem pavilion, where bumper cars playfully dodged each other and often crashed," wrote Kaslow, "[and] the Cuddle Up ride, where cups on saucers once swirled their human contents." She adds, "Sloping down toward the Potomac river is...the Crystal Pool. The grand entrance, topped off by a midnight-blue neon sign, befits a facility where 3,000 people once splashed together."

Thousands came to Glen Echo. Tommy Dorsey, Glenn Miller, and Woody Herman conducted their bands there. Future NBC weatherman Willard Scott broadcast shows from the park's glamorous Spanish Ballroom, which could hold more than 2,000 dancers.

But after World War II, affluent Americans left cities like Washington for distant suburbs. They forsook trolleys for autos. Instead of going out, they watched television. And while other parks kept attracting customers, Glen Echo actually refused them. The park was "Whites Only."

In 1961 the city council forced Glen Echo to admit Blacks, but bad feelings lingered. Glen Echo became dangerous, writes park expert Al Griffin. "Women were molested constantly; fights raged almost every weekend; and concessionaires were robbed."

On Easter Sunday, 1968, the park grew so overcrowded that its bosses shut it down. Frustrated youths attacked parts of the park. "On their way back to the city down tony Massachusetts Avenue, the youths threw rocks at houses," writes Kaslow. "That was the amusement park's last season."

The National Park Service took over Glen Echo in 1971. By 1995, the former funland had become a National Arts Park, offering puppet shows, carousels, and music. And the park that once barred Blacks was fully integrated.

**Old-time fun at
Palisades Park.**

Palisades Park

"You'll never know how good a kiss can feel/'Til you stop at the top of a Ferris wheel/And I fell in love/Down at Palisades Park."

With that lyric written by Chuck Barris and performed by Freddy Cannon, Palisades Park became immortal.

Built in 1898 on picnic grounds at the New Jersey palisades near the Hudson River, the park boasted "entertainment, nature, and colorful attractions." "The Palisades became one of America's favorite amusement parks," wrote journalist Patricia Hassler. Three hundred million people visited it.

The Palisades had the usual amusement-park attractions, such as a roller coaster and a tunnel of love. And it had entertainment. "Big names from Benny Goodman to the Jackson Five appeared at the park," Hassler wrote.

But Palisades was most famous for gimmicks. Hassler noted that the owners of Palisades "had a knack for letting the park reflect the culture of the nation. The austerity of the 1930s saw Kewpie-doll prizes replaced by coffee and sugar; the 1940s promoted beauty pageants such as Miss Eyeglass-Wearing [not to mention Miss Polish America and Miss Fat America]; the 1950s saluted rock and roll; the 1960s saluted rocket ships."

Other gimmicks were sleazier. "Palisades would both name a ride after practically any product or company that would come up with a $6,000 fee and distribute 35,000 samples of the product to the patrons," writes Al Griffin in *Step Right Up, Folks!*" "[It] used promotional tie-ins more than any other traditional park in the country.... In 1969, the captive audience was subjected to such promotions as Coca-Cola's Hi-C, Pepsi-Cola's Mountain Dew, Philip Morris' Clark gum, Luden's mint candies, Procter and Gamble's Top Job cleaner and Prell concentrate, Hormel's Spam, General Foods' Maxwell House coffee, and Quaker Oats' Cap'n Crunch cereal."

Even worse, Palisades attracted vandals. Soon, the park's neighbors were calling it "a gaudy nuisance."

In 1971, the Centex-Winston Corporation bought the park, razed it, and built apartments on its site.

Playland-at-the-Beach

"The West's Greatest Amusement Center," Playland-at-the-Beach called itself. "Mention the word Playland to any longtime San Franciscan, and their eyes light up," report authors Erika Lenkert and Matthew Poole in *Frommer's '97 San Francisco*. "They'll launch into a wealth of stories about fun and wild times at the city's bygone and beloved amusement park."

In the late 1800s, San Franciscans relaxed on a beach at the city's northwest end. Further south, at Ocean Beach (near today's Golden Gate Park), stood what Lenkert and Poole call "a shantytown of squatters." The squatters saw the crowds going north and "built a row of carnival stands that became equally, if not more, popular with beachgoers than the impressive neighboring establishments," say Lenke and Poole. "By the early 1900s, the squatters' carnival grew into a burgeoning amusement center."

Within a few years, Ocean Beach included a carousel, bumper cars, a Ferris wheel, and the formidable Big Dipper roller coaster. The Chutes, a splashy water ride, became a local institution. The funhouse featured the infamous Laughing Sal, a huge, mechanical woman who laughed so loudly that she scared kids. "Ocean Beach became the place to go," say Lenkert and Poole. "Elite and laymen alike swarmed here to picnic, play, hear jazz, ride the rides, eat at the dozens of restaurants, dance, and be seen."

George Whitney saw Playland and liked it. He was an amusement-park veteran, reportedly the inventor of the jumbo hot dog, the Photo-While-You-Wait booth, and the life-size cardboard caricatures where tourists stick their heads to get their pictures taken. He also became a real estate developer.

Whitney took over the site in the 1920s and professionalized it. "He allowed no ballyhoo in Playland-at-the-Beach, staffing his concessions instead with young employees working on salary," says amusement-park expert Gary Kyriazi. "Prizes for the games were coupons redeemable at the merchandise store.... Whitney's most popular prize was the Kewpie doll, of which he bought 300,000 a year." In the 1940s, he expanded Playland by a good 50 percent, making it what Kyriazi calls "the world's largest privately owned amusement park."

In the early '50s, however, high maintenance and insurance costs for the Chutes and Big Dipper cut Playland's bottom line. Whitney destroyed them. But without the two popular rides, Playland stopped attracting big crowds.

Whitney died in 1971. Shortly thereafter, another developer bought Playland in order to build "a small, beautiful urban community" on the site.

Playland was torn down in 1972. "There are thousands who fondly remember it," say Lenkert and Poole. "This wonderful place...not only brought joy to generations of San Franciscans but also played an essential role [in] developing the city as a fun-loving town."

Marineland of the Pacific

The Palos Verdes Peninsula is a fist of land bordered on three sides by the Pacific Ocean and on the fourth by Los Angeles and other cities. It was ideal for one of the most beloved entertainments of three decades: Marineland.

Just another day at Marineland.

Marineland was a theme park before Disney invented them. Opening in 1954, a year before Disneyland, the spread of more than 100 acres was the West's

first aquatic funland. Wrote Gary Kyriazi in *The Great American Amusement Parks* (published while Marineland was still open), "Marineland presents an amazing and highly entertaining series of aquatic shows, featuring performing dolphins, killer whales, sea lions, pearl divers, and 100-foot high-divers." Visitors could even strap on a snorkel and swim beside what the *Los Angeles Times*' Jack Cheever called "iridescent clouds of tropical fish." If they got tired of fish, visitors could always ride up the 300-foot Sky Tower or visit the Jungle Island.

Comparing Marineland to other sea parks, Kyriazi called it "the best of them all."

"Marineland has never refused to accept a stranded or injured sea mammal from the Humane Society or Animal Rescue League," wrote *Sea Frontiers* magazine's John C. Fine. "Past president of the American Cetacean Society Bill Samaras praised [the park's whale shows], emphasizing how they have contributed to the protection of whales."

But it was costly. Fine said, "Over one million gallons of water are pumped through its tanks daily, and 1,500 pounds of fish are consumed each day by Marineland tenants." The park also had up to 300 employees to pay.

Even worse, Disneyland and other parks drew customers away. From 1972 through 1986, the troubled Marineland changed owners four times. On December 30, 1986, the current owner, Warwick International, sold it to publisher and theme-park owner Harcourt Brace Jovanovich.

HBJ's Sea World parks starred killer whales. HBJ needed more of them, but new ones are hard to catch. Only Marineland had one that bred in captivity. HBJ moved it to San Diego's Sea World on January 20, 1987. Within two weeks, noting that "there is no way we can gain over 1 million paying attendance without killer whales" (Marineland needed 1.2 million visitors per year to make a profit), HBJ planned to shutter Marineland. The final wrecking ball swung 13 months later.

In 1995, real-estate developer Jim York, a fan of Marineland since childhood, bought the site. He said that he hoped to build a hotel and golf course there.

THE WONDERS OF LAS VEGAS
Dunes Hotel

The Dunes was one of the wildest rides in Las Vegas' wild history.

In 1955, Las Vegas was growing fast. The Dunes was "[the] third major hotel-casino to enter the fearful fray that fateful spring," says Vegas expert Deke Castleman. The $4 million, 85-acre Dunes, Castleman says, had "200 rooms, [a] 150-foot-long lagoon with an 80-foot V-shaped swimming pool (longest in the country at the time), and a 40-foot Sheik of Baghdad statue smiling down on the Strip."

Unfortunately, the Dunes' owners (who included an allegedly mob-connected theater owner) lacked casino experience. "All departments in the Dunes Hotel that fateful first month had been geared to lose [money], with the exception of the casino," writes journalist Ed Reid in *Las Vegas: City Without Clocks*. But many of the casino's customers paid in IOUs, checks, and markers, not the cash that the Dunes needed. "In six weeks, the Dunes had a huge backlog of such uncollected debts," Reid says. In 1956, the Dunes closed its casino—a shocking move in Vegas.

Enter some new investors. Within six months the casino was open again, and the Dunes inaugurated "Minsky's Burlesque," the Strip's first topless floor show. Minsky's brought in big crowds and turned the Dunes around.

Soon, the hotel added 250 more rooms and a golf course. In 1961, it began regular junkets from New York, which made it even richer. By 1965, it had more than 1,000 rooms and had added the world's tallest sign—"a gold and ruby abstract minaret soaring 22 stories [180 feet] into the sky," as art critic J. Hoberman described it.

The Dunes' fame attracted new groups of owners, and then other new groups. The frequent shifts in control didn't help the hotel: In 1985, it went bankrupt.

The hotel kept operating, but it stayed relatively static while its rivals were adding theme parks and other attractions. In 1992, for example, Hilton Hotels spent $100 million to spruce up and enlarge its venerable Flamingo.

The next year, Mirage Resorts bought the Dunes. In October, as 250,000 people watched, a British pirate ship shot a cannonball at the Dunes. The ship and ammo were fake, but the implosion that followed wasn't. Mirage owner Steve Wynn was blowing the Dunes to bits. On its site, he planned new hotels such as the pirate-themed Treasure Island at a cost of more than $1 billion.

The Dunes was gone, but its flamboyance was still rolling.

Landmark Hotel

Although the Landmark is gone, you can still see it. Go to the video store and rent the James Bond movie *Goldfinger*: A woman gets hurled out of the window of a hotel—not the Landmark—and lands in the Landmark's pool. Or *Casino*: Some of the movie was filmed there. Or *Mars Attacks!*: Director Tim Burton filmed the Landmark's destruction as if Martians were responsible.

The Landmark really was a landmark. The tallest building in Las Vegas was shaped like a 31-story mushroom. Its round casino topping a tower of hotel rooms offered an unmatched view of the city's gaudy lights.

Frank Carroll, a Kansas City builder who picked a spot across the street from Las Vegas' new convention center, borrowed $3 million and started building the Landmark in 1961. "By early 1963, Carroll, who wanted to erect the tallest building in Nevada, went broke in a height war with the Mint tower downtown," writes Vegas expert Deke Castleman in his book *Las Vegas*. "The Landmark sat, a half-finished shell, for the next three years."

With money from a Teamsters Union pension fund, Carroll finished the hotel, which did indeed outpoint the Mint (by seven feet). "By then, however, Carroll and his partners had long since run out of cash and credit, and the hotel immediately went up for sale," says Castleman.

Billionaire Howard Hughes bought it. The hotel finally opened on 1969's Independence Day weekend, with TV star Danny Thomas as the headliner. "For all the grand-opening excitement," Castleman says, "the Landmark immediately went back into decline, losing an estimated $5 million in the first week of operation."

Hughes' Summa Corporation later sold the Landmark, but none of the new groups of owners (there were quite a few over the years) could make it pay for long. In 1990 (according to Anthony Curtis, publisher of the newsletter *Las Vegas Advisor* and author of *Bargain City: Booking, Betting and Beating the New Las Vegas*), "a U.S. bankruptcy court action place[d] the Landmark in the hands of a federal trustee.... Location, design, and questionable management are blamed." The hotel limped along for less than two years and finally closed.

In November 1995, it blew up. A controlled implosion turned the hotel into a cloud of dust against the night sky. A parking lot replaced what was once the tallest tower in the world's most garish city.

Sands Hotel

In December 1952, Pope Pius XII called for "a more intense and multiplied love for the poor," but the revelers crowding the new Sands Hotel didn't care. "The hotel's original 200 rooms, contained by five two-story Bermuda-modern buildings named after race tracks and set in a semicircle around the pool...remained filled, continuously, for the rest of the decade," says Deke Castleman in his guidebook *Las Vegas*.

"The Sands itself reigned as the in place for glamour and style throughout the 1950s," Castleman says—largely because Frank Sinatra and Dean Martin each owned 9 percent of the hotel, and they performed in its Copa Room. Judy Garland, Jimmy Durante, Wayne Newton, Nat King Cole, Carol Burnett, Tallulah Bankhead, and Red Skelton did shows there, too. Other stars at the Sands included Milton Berle, Danny

Rat Packing it at the Sands with Frank, Dino, Sammy, Peter, and Joey.

Thomas, Lena Horne, and the members of Sinatra and Martin's famous Rat Pack. As *Wall Street Journal* reporter Bruce Orwall has written, "The Sands' Copa showroom defined Vegas-style lounge entertainment."

The Sands added 83 more rooms and suites in 1962 and doubled the size of the Copa Room and the casino in 1965. It sprawled over more than 60 acres.

Billionaire Howard Hughes bought the hotel in 1967 and cut off Sinatra's credit. Furious, Sinatra left the Sands and took his famous friends with him. The Sands' long, slow decline began.

Saudi arms dealer Adnan Kashoggi, sometimes called the world's richest man, liked to gamble. He'd easily win or lose up to a million dollars in a night. And he liked the Sands.

Accountant Steve Hyde, hired during 1981 as the Sands' chief executive, soon found that "the place depended on one player—Adnan Kashoggi." Investigative reporter David Johnston, in his book *Temples of Chance: How America Inc. Bought Out Murder Inc. to Win Control of the Casino Business*, quotes Hyde: "[Kashoggi] owed millions, but he didn't pay his markers, and the place went bust."

The Sands changed hands in 1988, then again in 1989. The newest owner, Sheldon Adelson, founded the huge Comdex computer show and helped the Sands by making it one of the show's hosts. But even Comdex wasn't enough.

In 1996, Adelson announced plans to demolish the Sands and build the Venetian, a $2 billion luxury resort.

OTHER PLACES
The Cotton Club

Duke Ellington performed there. So did Lena Horne (in a costume made only of three feathers) and Louis Armstrong, Ella Fitzgerald and Ethel Waters, Cab Calloway and Bill "Bojangles" Robinson, and Stepin Fetchit and Dorothy Dandridge. The standard "Stormy Weather" was written for one of its revues. Radio shows broadcast from there.

Even the audiences glittered. From Broadway came Noël Coward, Fred Astaire, Jimmy Durante, Ethel Merman, songwriter Irving Berlin, and producers Billy Rose and Flo Ziegfeld. From all over came FBI chief J. Edgar Hoover, ballplayer Babe Ruth, violinist Jascha Heifetz, and classical conductor Leopold Stokowski, who after an Ellington show said, "Now, I truly understand the Negro soul."

With all this dazzle came the Mob. After 1919's Volstead Act made alcohol illegal and thus ripe for criminal control, Hell's Kitchen gangleader, thief, and murderer Owney Madden reached for the nightclub business. He grabbed Harlem's Club Deluxe, which became the Cotton Club. It opened in 1923, presenting "an uptown version of the lavish Negro stage revues that were selling out theaters down on Broadway," writes historian Jim Haskins in *The Cotton Club: A Pictorial and Social History of the Most Famous Symbol of the Jazz Era.* Lena Horne has recalled, "The shows had a primitive, naked quality that was supposed to make a civilized audience lose its inhibitions."

Come to the Cotton Club!

"The exact derivation of the name Cotton Club is not known, but it is likely that the club's intended 'whites only' policy, together with intimations of the South, were behind the choice," Haskins notes. The audience stayed all-White until late 1928, when Ellington forced management to let the performers' Black friends and relatives see the shows.

While the Cotton Club gleamed, the Depression tortured the rest of Harlem. In March 1935, reports of a White man beating a Black teenager triggered a riot. Going to Harlem seemed less stylish to the few rich Whites left on the club circuit. On February 16, 1936, the Cotton Club closed.

A few months later, it reopened on Broadway and 48th Street, the heart of the theater district. All seemed well until 1939, when the federal government indicted the Cotton Club for tax evasion.

Moreover, as Haskins points out, "tastes in entertainment had changed. Lavish Ziegfeld-type shows were no longer as popular even on Broadway, and it followed that they could not last long in night clubs." On June 10, 1940, the Cotton Club shut down.

"Nostalgia has not played anyone false about the Cotton Club shows," Lena Horne has said. "They were wonderful."

Pennsylvania Station

It was a big idea, inspired by an entire continent.

When Pennsylvania Railroad chief Alexander Cassatt visited Europe, he saw mighty railroad stations such as Paris' Gare Montparnasse and "wanted to give his

Penn Station, the New York Colossus.

country her own symbol of progress," writes Lorraine Diehl in *The Late, Great Pennsylvania Station*. Experts would call his edifice at New York City's 33rd Street and 7th Avenue "civic architecture at its most effective" and "a triumph of style and emotion."

To make his masterpiece, Cassatt called on the prominent architectural firm McKim, Mead and White, which had designed much of Columbia University and did a major restoration on the White House. The job cost $112 million (close to a billion of today's dollars), took from 1903 to 1910, and covered 7½ acres of prime Manhattan real estate.

Penn Station was built to impress. Diehl describes "the 40-foot-wide Grand Stairway, at whose summit one could stand beside the bronze statue of Cassatt and gaze [at]...the most awesome interior space in the city." She explains, "The main waiting room of Pennsylvania Station...extended two city blocks.... The station's eight Corinthian columns, seven feet in diameter and 60 feet high, carried the eye in a breathtaking sweep...toward a coffered octagonal ceiling 150 feet high."

At the entrances stood eight 12-foot stone goddesses. Over the entire station perched 22 eagles, "more than five feet tall and weighing 5,700 pounds each," wrote the *New York Times*' Grace Glueck.

Penn Station was glorious, successful, and doomed. After World War II, Congress built highways, automakers increased production, car travel rose, train travel sunk, and the Pennsylvania Railroad suffered. "The railroad that had come out of the war in sound shape was now operating with a deficit that by 1951 reached $72 million," Diehl writes.

In 1960, the Madison Square Garden Corporation began planning a new complex to be built on Penn Station's site. The railroad, needing cash, accepted the idea. Architects protested and picketed, but on October 23, 1963, workers began killing Penn Station. Many of its statues and columns became landfill in New Jersey. Trains continue to operate beneath street level in what is still called Penn Station, but without the majestic old building that once stood above it.

"Now," Diehl says, "anyone who wants to connect with Alexander Cassatt's dream and Charles McKim's vision of a great railroad station will have to look for it in books. The station that they had dreamed about and built, the station that grew out of the power of the railroads and, more importantly, out of man's desire to express his spirit in stone, is gone."

A small part of the fabulous Roxy, 1927.

Roxy Theater

Life magazine called it "the big Manhattan movie mansion." The Roxy—named after its creator, Samuel "Roxy" Rothafel—was "a cavernous, gilded cathedral," according to biographer Neal Gabler in *An Empire of Their Own: How the Jews Invented Hollywood*. Its first paying customer, Herbert Pohl, said, "An air of great elegance prevailed throughout that theatre, and whoever talked dared not to do so but in whispers."

The Roxy Theater started out as a car barn on the corner of 50th Street and 7th Avenue in Manhattan. In 1925, film producer Herbert Lubin bought the space and made a deal with Rothafel ("the leading movie theater impresario in America," says Gabler) to build the world's greatest movie theater there. It cost $6 million.

The auditorium seated 6,000 people. Its loge section

included two life-sized bronze sculptures of ladies and cupids. The stage was 70 feet wide and so imposing that comic Joe Frisco said, "Don't ever get caught on the Roxy stage without bread and water."

The Roxy's huge Rotunda (Rothafel fired employees who called it the lobby) was 70 feet long, and topped by a vast dome with a 20-foot chandelier. On the marble floor lay what Rothafel called the world's largest oval rug: 58 feet by 41, weighing 2½ tons. The decor was "an exuberant grafting of Renaissance details on Gothic forms with fanciful Moorish overtones," according to Ben M. Hall, author of *The Best Remaining Seats: The Golden Age of the Movie Palace.*

The Roxy had a hospital, a menagerie, office suites, a laundry, a radio studio, 60 bathrooms, and five floors of dressing rooms. In addition to auditorium seating, it could fit 4,000 patrons (in the Rotunda) and employees (all over the theater). A Marine Corps colonel trained its ushers.

For years, the Roxy was a success. But when television supplanted movies, Rothafel's dream had a hard time hanging on. People preferred to stay home rather than fill Roxy's 6,000 seats night after night.

By 1960, the Roxy died. Wreckers demolished the place that Rothafel called "the cathedral of the motion picture."

London Bridge

...is not falling down. But it isn't there anymore, either.

"There" is London. And actually, London Bridge is there. But it's also in Arizona. Some explanations:

In A.D. 963, the early Brits began building the first known bridge over London's River Thames. It was made of wood and took 12 years to construct.

Centuries of London weather do awful things to wood. Although the bridge was updated and rebuilt, it was clear by 1176 that wood simply wasn't sufficient.

Peter of Colechurch, a priest who had overseen the last wooden bridge, designed a bridge of stone. It was a huge undertaking: 19 arches, each spanning 15 to 34 feet wide; massive piers resting on heaps of submerged rubble; a chapel; wooden shops and houses; and defensive towers. Construction took more than 30 years, ending in 1209.

The bridge was a wonder. It was the only passage over the Thames until the mid-1700s, when Westminster Bridge was constructed. Although it was rebuilt several times, and fires caused the removal of its shops and houses in the early 1760s, Colechurch's design and basic structure stayed in place for more than 600 years.

Still, nothing can be rebuilt and re-rebuilt and re-re-rebuilt forever. In 1831, London Bridge was demolished.

Yet London Bridge stood stronger than ever. Before the death of Colechurch's masterpiece, designer John Rennie created a new London Bridge, a five-arched masonry behemoth, 928 feet long. King William IV presided over its opening in 1831. It attracted so much traffic that it was widened in 1902 through 1904.

Traffic caused its removal. By the 1960s, author Hermione Hobhouse writes in *Lost London*, "Heavy lorries and other vehicles, of which some 50,000 a day were calculated to cross [the bridge], were causing settlement of the pier foundations."

London Bridge around 1900.

In 1967 and '68, London Bridge was dismantled. It was replaced by a new bridge, six lanes wide and made of concrete, perfect for auto traffic.

What about the old bridge? An American developer bought its facade and re-erected it in Lake Havasu City, Arizona, as a tourist attraction.

But don't look for it in London. It isn't there anymore.

The Brown Derby

"Eat in the Hat" commanded the sign above the Brown Derby, and thousands obeyed.

Herbert Somborn, second husband of movie star Gloria Swanson, opened the Brown Derby near Los Angeles' tony Ambassador Hotel in 1926. The hat was made of brown cement, complete with a gently rising brim and a "band" of windows.

"There are many tales of how the Derby got its shape," writes author Richard Alleman in his entertaining *The Movie Lover's Guide to Hollywood*. "One says that

The Brown Derby, 1952.

the building was inspired by New York Governor Al Smith—a friend of Somborn's—who was wearing a brown derby on a visit to Los Angeles. Another says that Somborn had been challenged by a friend who said: 'If you know anything about food, you can sell it out of a hat.' Then there are those who see the derby hat as being a symbol of upper-middle-class social acceptability. According to this you-are-where-you-eat theory, what could be classier than dining inside a derby?"

There were actually four Brown Derbies (though only one was shaped like a hat). The one most important in entertainment history stood in the heart of Hollywood, a few miles northwest of the hat. The Hollywood Brown Derby "was long the luncheon meeting place of the biggest stars of motion pictures and radio, because of its close proximity to so many studios and broadcasting stations," says *Take Sunset Boulevard: A California Guide* by Barbara and Rudy Marinacci.

There were two other Brown Derbies as well, one to the west in Beverly Hills and another to the northeast in the Los Feliz neighborhood. But the original, the one shaped like a hat, was the most famous.

Like much of Hollywood, the hat-shaped Brown Derby fell on hard times. In 1980, it closed and would have been demolished but for an outcry from concerned citizens. The Brown Derby was installed atop a nearby mini-mall. There is now a restaurant called the Brown Derby in Las Vegas' MGM Grand Hotel; but it, of course, isn't the original.

The other Brown Derbies changed hands and names, as Los Angeles real estate often does. For instance, the Los Feliz Brown Derby is now a dance club. Men and women in their 20s, dressed in sharp shirts and slinky skirts, crowd the floor and do the East Coast swing to music that was old before they were born. The name of the club is The Derby.

Studio 54

It was the capital of the night. Singers were there: Elton John, Rod Stewart, Liza Minnelli, Dolly Parton, Mick Jagger, Cher, Diana Ross, and a teenage Michael Jackson. And dancers like Rudolph Nureyev and Mikhail Baryshnikov. And artist-celebrity Andy Warhol.

Want to make political connections? President Carter's mother and his son Chip were there. So were Caroline Kennedy and Betty Ford, New York mayor Abe Beame and Virginia senator John Warner, Canadian first lady Margaret Trudeau and former Joe McCarthy aide turned power broker Roy Cohn. It was there that Israeli general Moshe Dayan danced with actress Gina Lollabrigida.

There were other actors, too: Elizabeth Taylor, Jacqueline Bisset, Ryan O'Neal, John Travolta. And athletes: O.J. Simpson, Tom Seaver, John McEnroe, Ilie Nastase.

Behind the bar at Studio 54. Note the bizarre flower arrangement.

And fashion figures: *Vogue*'s Diana Vreeland, models Cheryl Tiegs, Farrah Fawcett, and Brooke Shields (at age 11), and designers Halston, Calvin Klein, Diane Von Furstenberg, Betsey Johnson, and Karl Lagerfeld.

The club was so fame-heavy that on opening night, Jack Nicholson couldn't get in. "Among those who were excluded, at one time or another, were Frank Sinatra, the president of Cyprus, the King of Saudi Arabia's son...and several young Kennedys," says journalist Bob Colacello.

Studio 54 opened on April 26, 1977, after restaurateur Steve Rubell and his partner and attorney, Ian Schrager—whom one scenester called "two P.T. Barnum types"—bought a former CBS studio at 254 West 54th Street in New York and remodeled it. "A long, wide, dark entrance hall, its carpeted floor inclining upward, led to the big, round bar," Colacello reports. "The well-built young bartenders and busboys wore gym shorts and sneakers, and danced as they made and served drinks.... Beyond [the bar] was the 11,000-square-foot dance floor with its 85-foot ceiling."

The club threw lavish parties. It became a farm with live animals, a fantasy of Peking, and a baby land ("with busboys in diapers," Colacello says). It offered excesses, including promiscuity and drug abuse.

In December 1978, IRS agents raided Studio 54. They found cocaine, account ledgers (later used to prove income tax evasion), and stacks of cash. In January 1980, Rubell and Schrager were sentenced to 3 1/2 years in prison and fined $20,000 each. They sold the club. Studio 54 never regained its popularity and went out of business.

After prison, Rubell and Schrager went into the hotel business. Rubell wasn't to enjoy it: He died of AIDS in 1989.

But almost everyone who went to his dance hall concurs with the description that record executive and socialite Ahmet Ertegun gave it: "the greatest club of all time."

Red neon, a palm tree, and a famous name: It's the Hollywood star of pharmacies.

Schwab's drug store

Schwab's was Hollywood. Greta Garbo went there; so did Marlon Brando, James Dean, Lucille Ball, Errol Flynn, Elvis Presley, and tycoon Howard Hughes. The pharmacy's neon sign inspired songwriter Harold Arlen to write the classic "Over the Rainbow."

"Orson Welles used to sit at the fountain, unaware that the pharmacist behind him was occasionally on the phone to his nemesis, William Randolph Hearst," recalls Sondra Farrell Bazrod, daughter of Schwab's chief pharmacist. "Jack Nicholson, then undiscovered, spent many hours in the coffee shop. One day, when he was asked to leave because customers were waiting for a booth, he told Loma, one of the waitresses, 'Mark my words, I'm going to be a star, and no one will ever ask me to leave again.'"

What made Schwab's special? Part of it was timing. Lena Schwab and her pharmacist son Jack were already running a pharmacy several miles to the east, in downtown Los Angeles; but they moved to Hollywood in 1932, as the movies were booming.

Part of it was location. At 8024 Sunset Boulevard, Schwab's lay close to the home of luminaries from W.C. Fields to F. Scott Fitzgerald: the Garden of Allah, "the most famous and most star-studded apartment house anywhere in Hollywood," writes author John Pashdag in *Hollywoodland, U.S.A.: The Moviegoer's Guide to Southern California*. Nightclubs like Ciro's and the Mocambo were nearby. And, Bazrod says, "Dr. Frank Nolan, whose patients included [Marion] Davies, [Errol] Flynn, Rita Hayworth, and the Andrews Sisters, had his office next door."

Part of it was Schwab's itself. "There was something about the place, with its wood paneling and long, narrow interior, that seemed comforting," Bazrod says. Besides, it was the only place in miles open for breakfast at 7 A.M.

After show-biz columnist Sydney Skolsky started using Schwab's as his office—and after Lana Turner was allegedly discovered there (she wasn't, but she spent time there)—Schwab's became a hangout for Hollywood hopefuls. In Billy Wilder's *Sunset Boulevard*, William Holden calls it "a combination office, kaffee klatsch, and waiting room."

In the '60s, the movie studios declined, while rock 'n' roll clubs arose on Sunset. To the street's new, young crowd, Schwab's seemed old and fusty. Fights within the Schwab family tore the place apart.

Schwab's closed in 1983. "Everything from the neon sign to the pharmacy's Rolodex was auctioned off," writes Pashdag. The building was demolished in 1987.

Today, a Virgin Megastore stands on its site. Like Schwab's, the store is attractive and well-stocked. Like Schwab's, it's hosted celebrities, some of whom visit to promote their records. Like Schwab's, it sees plenty of aspiring performers, who pick through the extensive compact-disc selection.

But, sadly, it's not Schwab's.

all gone

Chapter Twelve

PLANES, TRAINS, AND OTHER HIGH-SPEED TRANSIT

Eastern Air Lines in flight.

Speed has characterized the 20th century. Except for visionaries like H.G. Wells and Alfred, Lord Tennyson, few people in the Victorian age foresaw airplanes, helicopters, diesel trains, space travel, and other leaps around the world. Rapid transit has developed so fast that vehicles once barely imaginable are now obsolete.

Obsolete, yes—but before they went under, they carved some pretty deep grooves in the tablets of world history. Western Airlines launched America's first ongoing regularly scheduled passenger service on May 23, 1926. "Passengers were furnished with an in-flight lunch, newspapers, market reports, magazines, and headsets with which to listen to radio broadcasts en route," says *Aviation History* magazine contributing editor C.V. Glines.

Despite successes—Western eventually flew to the West Coast, the northern midwest, the Rocky Mountain region, Hawaii, Alaska, Florida, Canada, and

Mexico—the federal government's deregulation of the airline industry in 1978 laid Western low by allowing younger, more aggressive competitors to spring up. In 1987, Delta Air Lines bought the tired, old company and eliminated it.

Or take Eastern Air Lines. Eastern originated shuttle service and became one of America's largest passenger carriers. But it too couldn't handle the deregulation of airlines, not to mention price-cutting competitors, union troubles, low employee morale, an expansion that racked up huge costs, and other problems. It went bankrupt in 1991.

Still, many people remember Eastern fondly. And that's true of a lot of the items in this section.

Hef with his friend Barbi Benton and a flight attendant aboard the Big Bunny to London, 1970

AIR AND SPACE TRAVEL
The Big Bunny

Hugh Hefner worked big. He dreamed up the Playboy empire; mansions in Chicago and Los Angeles; and the Big Bunny, corporate jet of Playboy Enterprises, Inc.

At over $5 million, the McDonnell Douglas DC-9 was the world's priciest private jet. All black on the outside except for the white Bunny logo on the tail, its real wonders were inside. "White fiberglass free-form walls give an 'apartment feeling' to the living-room discotheque, to the cardroom and to the bedroom, with its huge, elliptical bed covered in Tasmanian opossum," wrote journalist Henry Ehrlich in *Look* magazine. "There are also seven TV monitors, an eight-track stereo, and a video apparatus so advanced that color tape for it has not yet been perfected, a movie screen raised and lowered by buttons, two galleys with a capacity for eight-course dinners for 30, [and] a closet filled with expensive Bordeaux and Napa Valley wines."

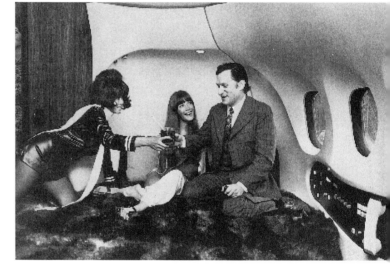

Hefner decided on the plane in 1968. "Hefner had been sequestered in the [Chicago] Mansion for more than five years," writes journalist Russell Miller in

Bunny: The Real Story of Playboy. "His weight had dropped from 175 to 135 pounds...he ate irregularly [and] never exercised." Hefner himself said, "I was killing myself. I had to get out of there."

A Los Angeles television producer asked Hefner to host a show called *Playboy After Dark.* He accepted, but arriving via commercial flight was not for him. Hence the Big Bunny.

Hefner and his chief Bunny Mother (who oversaw the Playboy Bunnies) picked 12 Bunnies and sent them to Continental Airlines for stewardess training. Architect Ron Dirsmith, who remodeled the Chicago Mansion, turned the Big Bunny into what *Newsweek* called "the most mind-boggling display of sensual opulence ever assembled in a flying machine."

Landing in Denver, Ehrlich reported, "the plane soon becomes the top sight-seeing attraction in town." Hefner rented the plane "to anyone who is willing to pay an estimated $1,140 an hour." He got few takers.

Far worse, the Drug Enforcement Administration in 1974 charged (wrongly) that the Big Bunny was used in drug trafficking. That same year, Playboy Enterprises, which had overexpanded, had to cut expenses. "The company's most extravagant and pointless expense [was] the Big Bunny, sitting in the sunshine in Los Angeles and eating up more than a million dollars a year," Miller writes.

An agonized Hefner sold the plane for about $4 million to the Venezuelan government. Reports Miller, "The lavish interior fittings were stripped out and replaced by rows of conventional aircraft seats; the fuselage was repainted white, and the flag of Venezuela was painted over the Bunny logo on the tail."

Skylab

A space station was a dream of stargazers for decades. Then, in 1973, it was real.

"NASA [National Aeronautics and Space Administration] had studied concepts for space stations...since the earliest days of the space program [in the 1950s]," says the NASA publication *Space Flight: The First 30 Years.* But only in the mid-'60s, when engineers created rockets strong enough to lift such a station, did the concepts become concrete.

Skylab aloft, 1973.

The 118-foot Skylab weighed about 100 tons, with about 1,000 cubic feet (equivalent to about 32 feet on a side) of habitable room. Three-men crews lived in that space for up to three months at a stretch—the longest American space flight up to that time and for years afterward.

On May 14, 1973, NASA launched Skylab, uninhabited. Seconds later (according to NASA's *The Early Years: Mercury to Apollo-Soyuz*), "atmospheric drag began clawing at Skylab's meteoroid shield. This cylindrical metal shield was designed to protect the orbital workshop from tiny space particles and the sun's scorching heat.... [With the shield gone] temperatures inside Skylab soared, rendering the space station uninhabitable."

The crew flew up to fix it. They set a Mylar "parasol" (which NASA engineers had quickly invented) over the area of the missing meteoroid shield, and Skylab cooled.

Skylab was manned for 171 days. The *Information Please Almanac* reports, "Three three-man crews visited the space station, spending more than 740 hours observing the sun and bringing home more than 175,000 solar pictures." They also studied Earth's natural resources and environment. Moreover, quoth the *Almanac*, "Skylab's biomedical findings indicated that man adapts well to space."

Between manned missions, Skylab stayed in orbit, 270 miles over Earth. After the last crew left in 1974, Skylab kept going.

In 1979, sunspot activity started to make the station's orbit decay sooner than NASA scientists thought it would. A few rounds shy of its 35,000th orbit, Skylab fell.

On July 11, 1979, at 12:37 P.M. Eastern Daylight Time, it hit the atmosphere. Most of it burned up from air friction; the parts that didn't crashed in Australia and the Indian Ocean. Fortunately, they hurt no one. After six years and $2.6 billion, Skylab was dead.

Was it worth the money and trouble? Rocketeer Werner von Braun thought so, years before Skylab was created. "Don't tell me man doesn't belong out there [in space]," he said. "Man belongs wherever he wants to go—and he'll do plenty well when he gets there."

People Express

After airline deregulation began in 1978, new airlines started sprouting like dandelions in spring. Perhaps the most prominent of them was the original no-frills American air service, People Express.

People Express began in 1980, the brainchild of executive Donald C. Burr. The Hambrecht and Quist investment group, which had made a fortune from Apple Computer and the Genentech genetic-engineering firm, raised $25 million to get the company running. From its base in Newark, New Jersey, People Express offered its first flights in 1981 and was a fast success.

People Express was an innovator, offering flights from Newark to Chicago for only $69 and from New York to Washington, D.C., for a startlingly low $19. How did it keep prices so tiny? "Short routes with small planes," explained the *New York Times'* Adam Bryant. Moreover, the company didn't bother much with costly, labor-intensive ticket counters; passengers were ticketed on the plane. And it charged only for the flight itself; to get coffee or baggage handling on People Express, you paid a separate charge.

In the recession of the early 1980s, when money was tight, People Express was seen as a godsend. It soon earned more than a billion dollars per year. The price of its stock took off like—well, like a jet.

Flush with money and confidence, People Express expanded. It offered more and more flights, including some overseas.

But the larger carriers didn't look kindly on the upstart that was stealing their passengers. The big guns installed computerized ticketing systems that allowed them to track and match People's prices. And the major airlines' prices, unlike People's, included full service. The big carriers began squeezing People and the other no-frills carriers that were competing for its business.

With its only advantage eliminated, and high costs mounting from its too-fast expansion, People Express suffered. The company went out of business in 1986.

"Our experience with People Express left us with a sense of 'If only...'" said Hambrecht and Quist chairman William Hambrecht. In 1994, he invested in a new no-frills carrier, Vanguard Airlines. Vanguard's boss was former People Express chief financial officer William McAdoo. Although the company doesn't go as far as People—

Cokes are included in the ticket price, for example—it carries on the low-fare tradition of People Express.

Braniff Airlines

It was like nothing else in the sky. Its planes were orange, green, and other colors, sometimes painted in wild swirls by famed artist Alexander Calder. Its seats had leather upholstery, and its lavish service outdid other carriers. It grew from a two-man concern, with a corporate secretary-treasurer who was also chief pilot, to America's seventh largest commercial airline.

And it dropped in one year from a net income of more than $45 million to a net loss of virtually the same amount.

Founded in 1930 by rich insurance man Tom Braniff and his brother Paul, a pilot, Braniff Airlines benefited from the 1938 Civil Aeronautics Act. To quote journalist and Braniff pilot John J. Nance in his book *Splash of Colors: The Self-Destruction of Braniff International*, the act "provided the operational latticework for the next 40 years and provided the legal and geographical structure—the operating rules and philosophies—under which two entire generations of airline managers and presidents would learn their craft."

Braniff prospered. By 1965, a Civil Aeronautics Board (CAB) member was calling Braniff "the most talked-about airline in America." From '65 to '76, Braniff's annual operating revenue grew fivefold.

But Braniff executives weren't ready when the Airline Deregulation Act of 1978 dismantled the latticework. Nance observes, "Deregulation, after all, demanded born-again entrepreneurs, but…the [1970s'] managers would know nothing of true, free-market airline management."

They tried. Braniff expanded, applying to the CAB for 626 new routes (it received 67) and hiring 588 new pilots. In one day—December 17, 1978—Braniff started operations in 16 cities that it had never served before.

Explosive expansion is expensive. In 1979 and '80, Braniff lost "an amount equivalent to every dollar of profit it had earned since January 1973," according to Nance. On May 12, 1982, Braniff went bankrupt.

The company didn't stay down for long—on March 1, 1984, Braniff (now owned by Hyatt Corporation) started flying again—but in 1992, after a second bankruptcy, the company went under for good. In 1995, the U.S. District Court in Brooklyn convicted former Braniff president Scot Spencer of taking $350,000 in kickbacks from Braniff's advertising agency and "concealing assets from the creditors during bankruptcy proceedings," according to the *Wall Street Journal.*

Most people who know Braniff prefer to remember its happier days, when its service was luxurious, its meals delicious, and its planes works of nearly psychedelic art.

TRAINS
Pacific Electric Red Cars

In the movie *Who Framed Roger Rabbit*, set in 1947, Hollywood detective Eddie Valiant uncovers a scheme to build something new: a freeway. Eddie can't believe it. "Nobody's gonna drive this lousy freeway when they can take the Red Car for a nickel!"

Eddie had a point. Angelenos loved the Red Cars, America's biggest interurban electric railroad. "Each day," wrote rail historian William Myers in *From Horse Car to Red Car to Mass Rapid Transit: A Century of Progress*, "over 6,000 scheduled trains carried patrons on 144 different local and intercity routes on a 1,100-mile network of trackage which extended into four southern California counties...."

In 1895, General Moses Sherman and his brother-in-law, Eli Clark, founded the Pasadena and Los Angeles Electric Railway (PLAER). It was Los Angeles' first electric intercity trolley line and one of the first in America. Henry Huntington, heir apparent to his uncle Collis' Southern Pacific railroad, bought PLAER and in 1901 renamed it the Pacific Electric Railway Company.

Pacific Electric laid scads of track. "Over these new routes ran a fleet of wooden-bodied trolley cars," Myers writes. "From the flamboyant gold-trimmed maroon paint job the trolleys sported, they soon received the nickname 'Big Red Cars.'"

By 1924, the PE was the biggest railway of its kind in the country. "Pacific Electric's vast system of interurban lines," wrote Robert McGonigal in *Trains Magazine* more than 70 years later, "helped create the sprawling megalopolis of greater Los Angeles."

But so did automobiles. "Worsening [traffic] congestion slowed down the Big Red Cars as they traveled along city streets to get to their private rights of way,"

Myers reports. Nor did the Depression help; people without money couldn't pay even the Red Cars' meager fares.

The PE didn't help itself in the 1940s, when it annoyed government officials by refusing to join regional transit plans. When freeways were built, they could have included rail lines—but in part thanks to the PE, they didn't.

Finally, there were (and are) dark rumors involving National City Lines, a firm founded by General Motors, Firestone, Standard Oil, and Mack Trucks. National bought street railways and destroyed them to encourage car and truck purchase. Some have speculated that National, or a similar conspiracy, helped to kill the Red Cars.

Red Car service ended on April 8, 1961. Mobs of Angelenos took one last ride. They would have agreed with Eddie Valiant's comment: "Who needs a car in L.A.? We got the best public transportation system in the world!"

Pullman train cars

It was the apex of lavish travel, a milestone in American labor relations, and its own city. It was a set of hotels on wheels that spawned Broadway shows and a classic movie.

In the late 1850s, George Mortimer Pullman started making sleeping cars, the sections of railroads where travelers spent the night. He raised the sleeping car (and the other cars that he would eventually build) to a level of luxury that few people, then or now, could have imagined.

A dining car with upholstery of tooled Spanish leather. Bridal stateroom suites with decor in cream and gold. Meals including Caviar Frais de Beluga, Coeur de Filet de Boeuf Coquelin, and Timballe d'Homard Grimaldi. Berth fronts of "Honduran mahogany ornamented with a classic wreath and love-knot motif," according to historian Lucius Beebe's *Mr. Pullman's Elegant Palace Car*. These were hallmarks of the best Pullman cars.

The all-Pullman Twentieth Century Limited inspired a hit play, a film with John Barrymore and Carole Lombard, and a

Inside a Pullman car.

155

stage musical. "At the height of its operation in the 1920s, the Pullman system welcomed to its berths and rooms more than 50,000 people nightly," writer Peter Maiken writes in *Night Trains: The Pullman System in the Golden Years of American Rail Travel*. Beebe adds, "Of all the sorts and conditions of beds occupied by Americans for a full century, more slept in Pullman berths than in any other."

Even more popular than Pullman's fittings was its service. "Giving each traveler pampered treatment—making him feel special—was the Pullman hallmark," say Patricia and Frederick McKissack, authors of *A Long Hard Journey: The Story of the Pullman Porter*. Maiken adds, "The Pullman porter was subjected to a training regimen and rule book that left nothing to chance (a commissary department instruction devoted five pages of text to the proper serving of a bottle of beer)."

These high standards came at a price. The residents of Pullman, Illinois—Pullman employees all—faced high retail prices (set by Pullman) and, in 1894, saw their wages cut. In a historic clash with management, the workers went on strike, losing the battle but inspiring thousands of rail workers nationwide to join unions. Porters formed their own union in 1925 to protest low wages and long hours. After 12 years of fighting, they won—the first Black union to do so against a major corporation.

Pullman stayed in business for decades after that, but passenger travel was shifting toward planes and cars. "On January 1, 1969, the one-time 'world's largest hotelkeeper' quit running Pullman cars," reports Maiken.

It was all over, except for the memories—and the occasional Broadway show.

Steam locomotives

"Even at rest, the steam locomotive is 'alive.' Its flanks radiate heat from the coal fire within, and it makes curious noises. The continuous high-pitched hiss-buzz of the turbine electric generator is muted from time to time by the click and thump of the air pumps (and the accompanying panting of exhaust steam into the stack) and the intermittent gargle of the boiler water injector. Whiffs of steam escape from odd spots around the engine, dripping condensate on the tracks below."

—Thomas H. Garve, *The Last Steam Railroad in America*

For 130 years the whistle in the night of the steam train meant travel and excitement. Ron Ziel and Mike Eagleson say in the book *Twilight of World Steam*, "For six generations, the destiny of America and especially of her young boys was irrevocably coupled to the romantic pageant of the steady parade of main-line steam power that marched incessantly through virtually every sizable hamlet and city."

Although steam trains were invented in England, the United States' trains led the world. Victor Hand, a railroad manager and author on rail topics, has said, "The railroads of North America built and operated the largest and most awesome steam locomotives the world has ever seen." At one point, 66,000 steam trains crisscrossed the nation.

Then came diesel. Though invented in 1892, the diesel engine didn't catch on fully in America until after World War II. By that time, trucks were hauling freight, while new cars and airplanes attracted passengers. Faced with this competition, historian Albro Martin writes in his book *Railroads Triumphant: The Growth, Rejection and Rebirth of a Vital American Force*, "The railroads gave everything they had, or nearly, to the effort to reestablish themselves as vigorous enterprises with a bright future. They heavily rebuilt and greatly improved their physical plant"—and that meant switching to diesel.

Steaming along in the mountains.

By 1970, it was all over for American steam. "The Denver & Rio Grande Western, the last sizable American all-steam line, ran its last freights on August 28–30, 1968," write Ziel and Eagleson. Other countries were dieselizing, too. India, the last major nation known for steam, was in the 1990s running only a few steam lines.

But the romance of steam still lives. Steam enthusiasts, who preserve old trains, still dream of that lonely whistle in the night.

all gone

Chapter Thirteen
READING

A hero in Ruritanian costume, a heroine showing lots of leg, and the lavender vine of death. Now, that's pulp!

Ever since the coming of radio and movies, pundits have complained that these new media will crowd print out of public consciousness.

Surprise! People still read. But some of the things that they read are gone.

Take Big Little Books. These things were tiny in every way except one: they were thick, with lots and lots of very small pages. "During the 1930s, Big Little Books became extremely popular at the dime stores," write Robert Heide and John Gilman in *Cartoon Collectibles: 50 Years of Dime-Store Memorabilia*. "These small books measure 3¾ inches to 4 inches wide and 4½ inches high. They are generally 300 to 400 pages in length, with the left-hand page containing the text and the right consisting of a drawing illustrating the text.... Sturdily constructed, with bright, colorful comic graphics on the thick cardboard covers, these 'novel-books with illustrations' were designed to fit snugly into a child's jacket pocket."

For an older (if not necessarily more mature) audience, there was *Captain Billy's Whiz-Bang*. "A mimeographed joke-and-cartoon paper," author Roy Thomas has called it. *Whiz-Bang* first appeared in 1919, published by Captain Bill Fawcett, sold half a million copies a month within half a year of its launch, and kept going for decades. Pulp-magazine aficionado Jim Steranko says that it was "named after a powerful artillery shell," but the name wasn't as important as the content. It had a reputation for raciness; in the Broadway hit *The Music Man*, slick-talking huckster Harold Hill uses it as an example of the corruption engendered by the presence of a pool table in town.

For adolescents of all ages, there were the bloody pulps. The pulp magazines (named for their cheap paper) were the birthplace of Tarzan, Zorro, Conan the Barbarian, and Dr. Kildare. With titles like *Spicy Mystery*, *Weird Tales*, and even *Medical Horror Stories*—and covers featuring lurid paintings of rugged men, voluptuous women, and bizarre danger—the pulps promised fast, visceral excitement. They also included early work by writers such as Ray Bradbury and Raymond Chandler. At their peak (before competition from comic books and television killed them off) there were more than 200 pulps with more than 20 million readers, nearly a fifth of the United States' population.

Another big-circulation creation was *Confidential* magazine. Introduced in 1952, *Confidential*—subtitled *Tells the Facts and Names the Names*—exposed private lives with a rapacity that the *National Enquirer* can only envy. "Why Sinatra is the Tarzan of the Boudoir," "Mae West's Open Door Policy," "Letter from a Hollywood Call Girl: I'll Take Danny Kaye at the Drop of a Hat": These were *Confidential*'s headlines, and its slangy stories lived up to them.

Confidential sold in the millions; some of its most devoted readers were movie people. "Everyone reads *Confidential*, but they deny it," said Humphrey Bogart. Others, including stars Maureen O'Hara, Liberace, and Errol Flynn, sued for libel, as did the state of California. The publisher, Robert Harrison, didn't care—he considered lawsuits publicity—but eventually the suits forced the magazine out of the scandal business. Its circulation dropped, and it vanished from newsstands.

Ah, the gentle art of reading. Nothing like it in the world.

Collier's magazine

Collier's published Winston Churchill and H.G. Wells, F. Scott Fitzgerald and Alfred Hitchcock, Agatha Christie and George Bernard Shaw, not to mention ballplayer Babe Ruth, movie star Douglas Fairbanks, football coach Knute Rockne, rocket scientist Werner von Braun, and boxer Gene Tunney. It offered eyewitness accounts of the 1906 San Francisco earthquake by Jack London, Lizzie Borden's ax-murder trial, the sinking of the *Titanic* by one of the passengers, and life in a Nazi death camp. Its attacks on patent medicines helped to pass the Pure Food and Drug Act and establish the Food and Drug Administration.

Launched by publisher Peter Fenley Collier (whose family would also publish

Collier s on the newsstand.

Collier's Encyclopedia), the first issue was dated April 12, 1888, and cover-billed "Fiction•Fact•Sensation•Wit•Humor•News." For nearly 70 years, it was all of that.

And feisty, too. "The sweetness-and-light story generally got the back of the hand from *Collier's* action-loving editors," notes its last editor, Kenneth McArdle. By 1914, the magazine "had a dozen crusades running simultaneously" against child labor, shoddy journalism, monopolistic trusts, "and any other handy targets."

The public loved *Collier's*. "By January 1920, the magazine was over 100 pages in size, and circulation was into the second million," McArdle reports.

And then, collapse. "For reasons involving changes of editors and a spectacular decline of editorial vitality...the issue of April 16, 1921, was down to 28 pages," says McArdle. Soon, new magazines, such as *Life*, pulled readers away. "The magazine flopped around, searching for a new soul and a new reason for being."

Some of the strategies worked. By the 1950s, according to the tome *Nostalgia: Our Heritage in Pictures and Words*, edited by Baldwin Ward, *Collier's* circulation was hitting an all-time peak.

But production costs were high and advertising revenue (the life blood of most magazines) was low. With the issue of January 4, 1957—featuring "Winter Vacations to Fit Your Budget," "Special Report on NON-Delinquency: 18,000,000 Teen-Agers Can't Be Wrong!" and "Princess Grace Prepares for Her Baby"—*Collier's* went under.

McArdle offers the best way to remember *Collier's*: "In a vigorous lifetime of 70 years, *Collier's* gave the American people a full measure of 'fiction, fact, sensation, wit, humor, and news.'"

New York Herald Tribune

First came the *Herald*, which publisher James Gordon Bennett started in 1835. "The paper virtually discovered Wall Street, and it led in financial news," wrote *Herald Tribune* journalist Fred Shapiro in *American Heritage* magazine. "It was also the first paper to give serious coverage of crime news, and…it was unexcelled in foreign coverage." The paper's writers included Mark Twain. It sent Henry Stanley to Africa to find missing missionary David Livingstone; when they met, Stanley uttered the famous line, "Dr. Livingstone, I presume?"

Even more prestigious was the *Tribune*, which ex-printer and eventual presidential candidate Horace Greeley opened in 1841. "The Bible of the West," distributed nationwide, printed Twain, Karl Marx, Henry Wadsworth Longfellow, Charles Dickens, Edgar Allen Poe, Walt Whitman, and Henry James—often as journalists, often before they were famous. Nor was the *Tribune* only a litterateur's paper. It broke such hot stories as the effort of 1876 Democratic presidential nominee Samuel Tilden to buy electoral votes.

But the early 1900s' sensationalistic "yellow journalism" drew lower-class readers from the two papers. Soon, says Shapiro, "[The *Herald*] and the *Tribune* were knocking each other out in competition for the same [affluent] readers." Result: The *Tribune* bought the *Herald*.

The merged *Herald Tribune* developed a stellar corps of writers, including the nationally syndicated humorists Art Buchwald and Robert Benchley, sportswriter Red Smith, pundits Joseph Alsop and Walter Lippmann, and chroniclers of American life Jimmy Breslin and Tom Wolfe. Reporters Marguerite Higgins and Homer Bigart won Pulitzer Prizes for their coverage of the Korean War.

By the 1960s, though, the *Herald Tribune* was under assault. Television had drained off the newspaper audience. Moreover, the Trib had troubles with its printers' union. "There was a 114-day strike in 1962, a ten-day shutdown and threats of others in 1965," Jimmy Breslin later wrote in *Life* magazine. The paper lost readers and revenues.

The *Trib*'s owner, John Hay Whitney, entered into a merger with the *New York World-Telegram* and *Journal American*, but it was too late. The *Herald Tribune* published its last edition on April 24, 1966. Only its Paris edition, the *International Herald Tribune*, survived.

"It was ten [o'clock] on Saturday evening, April 23, 1966, when M.C. (Inky) Blackman, a short, gray-haired rewrite man…finished the news story that was to be the *Tribune*'s final word," wrote Shapiro. "True to *Tribune* tradition, it was well written. Fittingly, it was an obituary."

Index Librorum Prohibitorum

Artist Joe Orlando remembers moving to a new home in Queens and receiving a courtesy call from the local Catholic pastor, who offered to bless his new home, room by room. Soon, they arrived at his upstairs studio, where the priest commented on Orlando's large collection of reference books, asking if he was careful to make sure that none were to be found on the Librorum Prohibitorum, or Catholic Index of Prohibited Books. Orlando assured him that he doubted that any were. [Orlando recalls,] "Then he said, 'Ah! You're an artist—and who do you work for?' I said, '*Mad* magazine,' and he said, 'That's on the Index!'"
—Maria Reidelbach, *Completely Mad: A History of the Comic Book and Magazine*

In addition to *Mad*, the Index included *Madame Bovary, Les Miserables*, works by Voltaire, Sartre, Zola, Molière, and Descartes (the French seemed to annoy the Index), plus *Decline and Fall of the Roman Empire* and other classics. For nearly 400 years, it listed the works that Catholics dare not read.

The Protestant Reformation sparked the Index. Condemning heresy wasn't new—journalist Brian Doyle notes in *U.S. Catholic* magazine that Pope Gelasius I published a list of forbidden works in A.D. 496—but Protestantism was. To fight it, Pope Paul IV (1555–1559) drafted the Index. "[Catholics] were barred from reading religious publications of non-Catholics," says theologian James Tunstead Burtchaell in the anthology *Modern Catholicism: Vatican II and After*.

The pious burned thousands of books. Reading Indexed works became a sin that could bring excommunication. The Vatican's Holy Office, in charge of the Index, added to the list until it included thousands of items, not all of them theological.

The Index was hard to enforce, thanks to Johann Gutenberg. The printing press that he invented in the 1450s allowed publishers to create too many books for the Church to examine and too many copies for anyone to burn.

Besides, the Index was hard to consult. *Time* magazine reported, "Even many Catholic college libraries do not have a copy."

In the 1960s, the revolutionary Second Vatican Council instituted many reforms, among them the abolition of the Index. "I cannot imagine that it is mourned by many, even among the most conservative Catholics," Doyle wrote in 1997. "A vibrant, dense, joyous faith of any stripe is one which punctures immorality and bad theology, not flees from it or locks it away."

Police Gazette

Keep the *National Enquirer*, tabloid TV, and shock-jock radio. The daddy of them all was the *National Police Gazette*.

Born in 1845, the pink-covered *Gazette* became America's longest-running weekly illustrated magazine. Its goal was "to assist the operations of the police department" by printing "a most interesting record of horrid murders, outrageous robberies, bold forgeries, astounding burglaries, hideous rapes, vulgar seductions, and recent exploits of pickpockets and hotel thieves."

The *Gazette* did even more. "It thoroughly covered the sporting scene in the days before athletics became a major industry," says Theodore Peterson, author of *Magazines in the Twentieth Century*. While other periodicals followed Victorian propriety, the *Gazette* "was happiest with a melodramatic tale of illicit love, such as 'Harlot's Revenge,'" according to author Ralph Andrist's *American Century: One Hundred Years of Changing Life Styles in America*. And it loved stunts: The *Gazette* "promoted competitions of every kind imaginable," journalist James Cox wrote in *Smithsonian* magazine. "There were contests for steeple climbing, oyster opening, hair cutting, one-legged dancing, sculling, and female pugilism."

By 1885, the *Gazette*'s circulation topped 100,000. By 1900, copies filled cigar stores, saloons, barbershops, billiard halls, and other manly places.

Unfortunately for the *Gazette*, publishers William Randolph Hearst and Joseph Pulitzer began filling their daily newspapers with wilder stuff than the weekly *Gazette*, and for a lower price. New magazines such as *Captain Billy's Whiz-Bang* offered racier stories than the *Gazette*. Liberated women from suffragettes to flappers invaded men's hangouts, making men self-conscious about the prurient *Gazette*. Lastly, the Depression hit.

By 1932, the *Gazette* was broke. A publisher known for sleaze bought it but didn't help it. Circulation fell to 20,000.

In 1935, ex-newspaperman Harold Roswell bought the magazine. "Roswell pushed circulation to what it had been in the magazine's heyday by converting the publication into a slick-paper monthly and by periodically overhauling its editorial approach to its raw ingredients, which in essence were the same mixtures as before," says Peterson. "In the early '60s, the *Police Gazette* was still around with Roswell listed as editor and with a following of about 175,000."

Competition remained tough, though. Skin magazines like *Playboy* had more sex; tabloids like the *National Enquirer* delved into scandal with more relish. The *Gazette* looked antiquated. It finallly died in the mid-1970s.

Today, it's almost impossible to find an old copy of the *Gazette* in even the manliest hangouts. But as long as the press covers sex, crime, and vice, the spirit of the *Police Gazette* lives on.

Look magazine

The temptation in describing *Look* is to compare it with *Life*. The two picture magazines had a lot in common, but they didn't start out that way.

In his book *The Great American Magazine*, *Life* staffer Loudon Wainright describes *Look*'s first issue: "Scenes from Japanese houses of prostitution, a picture of a bull seeming to bite a bullfighter, a story about hermaphrodites called 'When is a Woman Actually a Woman?', [and] newsreel clips showing an automobile skidding and killing a pedestrian," plus doctored celebrity photos. Author Charles Panati wrote in his book *Everyday Origins of Extraordinary Things*, "[*Look*] was printed on cheaper paper [than *Life*] and focused on personalities, pets, foods, fashions, and photo quizzes," while *Life* pursued somewhat more news-oriented stories.

"*Look* actually evolved from the Sunday picture section of the Des Moines, Iowa, *Register* and *Tribune*," Panati says. "In 1925, the paper surveyed its readers and discovered that they preferred pictures to text. Thus, the newspaper began running series of photographs." *Register* and *Tribune* publisher Gardner (Mike) Cowles envisioned a magazine of such pieces.

Cowles asked *Time* magazine publisher Henry Luce for financing. Luce didn't mind backing Cowles. Time Inc.'s *Life* would surely attract competitors, and as a Time Inc. memo observed, "We should protect our flanks with friendly cooperative enterprises

Look in 1958, covering baseball, Russia's Khrushchev, and the music business.

[e.g., *Look*], which will tend to discourage less desirable competitors." If *Look* made money, its investors—such as Time Inc.—would get some of it. And *Look*, being racier than *Life* and monthly (*Life* was weekly), would hardly compete with Luce's magazine.

Yet shortly after launching *Look* in 1937, Cowles turned against titillation. *Look* began to resemble *Life*; it went from monthly to biweekly; and Cowles bought back Time's share of *Look*. His magazine became a success that lasted for decades.

But it was expensive to print and promote. In 1971, burdened by high costs, *Look* died.

A few years later, French publisher Daniel Filipacchi revived *Look* and hired *Rolling Stone* editor-publisher Jann Wenner to run it. In *Rolling Stone Magazine: The Uncensored History*, author Robert Draper writes, "The *Look* that Jann Wenner inherited was losing half a million dollars per issue. Two issues into the enterprise, the Wenner-operated *Look* was economically profitable." Nonetheless, in 1979, Filipacchi killed *Look*.

Having died twice, *Look* may look like a double failure. Still, the memory of the Sunday supplement that fought the powerful *Life* has stayed with its readers for decades.

Walter Winchell's reporting

"The most famous columnist in America and in the world," *New Yorker* journalist Harold Brodkey called him. Biographer Neal Gabler has said, "By one estimate, 50 million Americans—out of an adult population of roughly 75 million—either listened to his weekly radio broadcast or read his daily column, which, at its height in the late '30s and '40s, was syndicated in more than 1,000 newspapers; it was, according to one observer, the 'largest continuous audience ever possessed by a man who was neither politician or divine.'"

Newsman Walter Winchell givin' it to 'em straight.

Bob Hope admitted that Winchell inspired his quick-talking comedy style. "Movie stars—Cagney and Bogart—modelled their styles and their approaches to roles and their voices on his persona," Brodkey added.

It wasn't only actors who admired him. "Winchell is the greatest newspaper-man that ever lived," said Ernest Hemingway, himself a former newsman. Historians Louis Snyder of the City College of New York and Richard Morris of Columbia University wrote, "He has done more to rouse the conscience of America against intolerance and totalitarianism than any other journalist of his time."

Winchell's slangy, fast-paced reportage mixed Broadway gossip, political commentary, and news about mobsters. His newspaper columns and rat-a-tat radio commentary spewed news like a machine gun, reaching 50 items in a short column or 230 spoken words per minute. Says Brodkey, "[FBI chief] J. Edgar Hoover is said to have assigned agents to listen to Winchell, because he had so much information."

And influence. In the '30s, Winchell's support of President Franklin Roosevelt and screeds against Adolf Hitler swayed public opinion. In a 1939 broadcast, Winchell commanded Louis Lepke, Public Enemy Number One, to turn himself in. Lepke obeyed, surrendering not to the cops or the FBI but to Winchell, who gave him to Hoover.

But journalism was changing. "The Luce magazines [*Time* and *Life*] imitated Winchell's tactics and improved on them," Brodkey writes. Moreover, radio's power was declining, but Winchell couldn't turn to television; he was visibly awkward and uneasy on the tube.

Winchell supported Senator Joseph McCarthy's losing anticommunist crusade, and became isolated politically. Newspapers by the hundreds canceled his column. In 1967, he ran a full-page ad in *Variety* "pleading with any New York newspaper...to publish his columns," reports his ghostwriter, Herman Klurfeld.

Winchell's raw-meat approach ("I'm the man who invented the low blow," he said) lived on in everything from talk radio to supermarket tabloids. But Winchell did not. On February 20, 1972, the most influential voice in modern American journalism died.

Photoplay magazine

Before the tube gave us Siskel, Ebert, *Entertainment Tonight*, and E! Entertainment Television, movie magazines had clout. And the queen of the breed was *Photoplay*.

The first and longest-lived movie magazine, *Photoplay* spent nearly 70 years offering lush portraits of the stars, peeks (albeit often fictionalized ones) into Hollywood's private lives, and cover lines that screamed glamour, mystery, and romance: "The Man All Hollywood Fears," "Latest Beauty Fads of Hollywood Stars," and "Hollywood's New Look in Sex."

According to *Starstruck: The Wonderful World of Movie Memorabilia* by Robert Heide and John Gilman, *Photoplay* began in 1911 as "an entertainment leaflet...with a circulation of 12,000," which the W.F. Hall Printing Company acquired as payment for a bill. Hall hired James Quirk, "an editorial sharpshooter who had pulled other magazines, such as *Popular Mechanics*, out of the red."

For a few years, *Photoplay* was "a more or less sober chronicle of motion picture activity," writes film critic Richard Schickel in *D.W. Griffith: An American Life*. Soon, it added gossip and behind-the-scenes reporting.

By 1922, *Photoplay* had two million readers. Soon, says Schickel, *Photoplay* had become "the most influential motion picture journal for the general audience." According to *Starstruck*, "The magazine had become so powerful that a studio could not afford not to advertise a new picture or publicize a star between its covers." Its writers included F. Scott Fitzgerald, H.L. Mencken, and Theodore Dreiser.

In 1932, at age 48, Quirk died of heart failure, but *Photoplay* kept going. It had dozens of competitors—*Modern Screen*, *Silver Screen*, *Screenland*, *Hollywood*, and more—and led them all in sales.

But in 1952, the scandal magazine *Confidential* blasted out raw exposés that made *Photoplay*'s tales of glamour look tame. Tabloids such as the *National Enquirer* aggressively splashed their covers with racy gossip. In 1974, *People* magazine came along for readers who liked their gossip with a bit of respectability. Blocked by these publications and their imitators, *Photoplay* went under in 1980.

It wasn't dead entirely. In their book *Going, Going, Gone: Vanishing Americana*, Susan Jonas and Marilyn Nissenson write, "The overwhelming success of a special edition in 1977 when Elvis died suggested that the publishers could keep their title alive by producing other occasional one-shots. In the years that followed, *Photoplay* reappeared to commemorate events like John Lennon's death or Michael Jackson mania."

But as a regularly published magazine that fed the fantasies of millions, *Photoplay* had faded to black.

all gone

Chapter Fourteen

SCHOOL AND OFFICE

"Change or die" should be the motto of most places of business, including schools. The need to cut costs and keep up with new developments forces businesses to change remarkably fast.

Computerization has forced many changes. Magazines and newspapers used to create pages by printing out strips of typeset text, painting the back of it with rubber cement (or running it through a hot-wax machine), and sticking it onto a board: the process called pasteup. Today, publishers compose pages on screen, eliminating such pains as torn type strips or uneven columns.

To make sure that the columns were straight, production artists used a T square. A T square is a long straightedge (called the blade) made of wood or steel, connected at right angles to a metal or plastic crosspiece with one straight side and one curved side (the head). The blade, which ranged from 18 to 60 inches long, was sometimes encased in transparent plastic so that the person using the T square could see the lines running under it. Because the blade was longer than the head, the tool was shaped like a letter T—hence its name.

Comic-strip artists, sign letterers, architects designing buildings—anyone who had to draw boxes (that is, squares) or parallel lines—they all used T squares. Cartoonist-teachers Dick Giordano and Frank McLaughlin add, "When held at the bottom end and placed over the shoulder at the proper angle, it makes a great back scratcher." But a computer with the right software can draw lines more perfect than any T square, with much less trouble and no need to erase if you make a mistake.

Computerized efficiency and convenience have also eliminated the old-fashioned sign-in registers at many hotels. Before computers came along, you checked into a hotel by writing your name (or an alias, if you were rooming with someone other than your spouse) in a large book at the registration desk. Although some hotels still keep registration books, they're clearly on the wane.

Another simple device butted out by technology was the doctor's mirror. Before penlights arrived to help a doctor to see into mouths and ears, many a physician strapped a mirror to his head. As he peered through the hole in the mirror's center, the silvery glass reflected the light of the examining room into whatever dark bodily crevice the doctor wanted to check.

Among the many items not found in schools anymore, inkwells were once found on thousands of desks. Before ballpoints, students put ink on their penpoints by dipping them into the little black receptacles. And if a girl wore long braids, she had to watch out: The young boy seated behind her might dip her hair into the ink, just for the heck of it.

Not all items faded because something better came along—some were found to be unsafe. The 1950s and '60s were the heyday of the round-cornered metal lunch box, emblazoned with pictures of TV stars, comic-book heroes, and other icons, or sometimes just a simple red plaid pattern. Unfortunately, boisterous kids used the hard, metal objects to bang each other around, inflicting head wounds and other traumas. Under public pressure, manufacturers shied away from metal lunch boxes. In most areas, the dangerous little devils are just plain gone.

Generally, though, new technology forced the old ways out. Today's state-of-the-art equipment is tomorrow's trash.

CALCULATING AND COMPUTING
Slide rules

"Anyone who can't use a slide rule is a cultural illiterate and should not be allowed to vote."

—Engineer-novelist Robert Heinlein in *Have Space Suit—Will Travel* (1958)

Many numerous professionals have shared Heinlein's viewpoint. The slide rule was their magic wand.

A slide rule is three bars, each bearing numbers marked by lines, like a ruler. Around the bars is a glass or plastic band (called the indicator) that displays a thin line

The engineer's best friend, circa 1950s.

from the rule's top edge to the bottom. The middle bar slides between the other two, and the indicator slides over all three.

To multiply, say, two times three, the user pushes the middle bar (the slide) until its number one sits directly over the lower bar's number two. He slides the indicator until its hairline lies over the middle bar's number three. Directly beneath, on the lower bar, is the answer: the number six.

Slide rules could handle almost any numbered job. Rule maker Keuffel & Esser declared, "[Slide] rules have... been made specially for chemistry, surveying, artillery ranging, steam and internal combustion engineering, hydraulics, reinforced concrete work, air conditioning, and other specialized fields."

Mathematician Edmund Gunter created the numbered bars in 1620. The next year, his colleague William Oughtred put the bars together to invent the first slide rule.

Digit heads loved it. Mechanical engineer F.A. Halsey wrote in the 1880s, "As a saver of time and mental wear in tedious calculations, its value is great and unquestionable."

It stayed popular. In the 1964–65 sales year, more than a million rules were sold.

Then came 1972 and the handheld calculator. John Heath, customer service manager at the slide-rule maker Sterling Plastics, described the effect on sales: "It was a downhill sleigh-ride."

Within a decade, slide rule making ended. Slide rules became collector's items. Collectors Robert Otnes and Roger Shepherd formed the Oughtred Society in 1991 to celebrate the tool. A 1992 auction in Köln, Germany, sold a 19th-century rule for $863. And in the book *Toolies*, engineer and humorist Stephen Clark wrote, "The time when any master toolie [Clark-speak for engineer] could be recognized by his leather-cased, finely crafted 'slip stick' hanging proudly from his belt is now just a memory."

Computer punch cards

"Do not fold, spindle, or mutilate." The phrase appeared on millions of cards that fed computers. To many people, it symbolized the idea that they should serve machines.

Around 1801, Frenchman Joseph-Marie Jacquard used cards to program a loom. "As the cards, which were strung together into a kind of tape, moved through a mechanical reader, wooden plungers passed through the holes, orchestrating the machine's operation," says computer journalist Stan Augarten in *Bit by Bit: An Illustrated History of Computers*. The cards changed the textile field and inspired Jacquard's contemporary, computer pioneer Charles Babbage. "We may say most aptly that the Analytical Engine [a computer that Babbage proposed] weaves algebraical patterns just as the Jacquard-loom weaves flowers," said Augusta Ada Byron, Babbage's partner.

Unfortunately, Babbage and Byron needed more than cards. The technology to make computers didn't exist yet.

In 1880, American census worker Herman Hollerith was annoyed that tabulating the census took months of slow calculations. A top census official, John Billings, may have known about the Jacquard loom; he may have been inspired by railroad conductors' ticket punching. In any case, he suggested punch cards to Hollerith; Hollerith developed them, and 1890's census tabulated three times faster than 1880's. Hollerith founded the Tabulating Machine Company, later changed to International Business Machines (IBM).

IBM sent cards everywhere. The manila-colored little devils, 7¾ inches by 3⅛, became the standard for machines worldwide.

They were also a nuisance. One punch out of place, one card folded or spindled or mutilated could render a program of several hundred cards useless.

Then came magnetic tape, which could store information in less space than the bulky cards. "By 1949," according to Time-Life Books' *Understanding Computers: Input/Output*, "IBM's management had approved a study of magnetic tape, to determine how much a threat the new medium posed to [punch cards]."

Tape proposed so big a threat that IBM didn't fight it. In 1952, IBM produced a computer that used both cards and tape.

With the personal computer revolution of the 1970s, which used magnetic tape discs, punch cards were dead. Americans could fold, spindle, and mutilate all they wanted.

UNIVAC

The University of Pennsylvania didn't know it, but it was a matchmaker to techno-parents. At UP, in the summer of 1941, lab instructor J. Presper Eckert taught electronics to student John Mauchly.

"Mauchly was forever experimenting with different technologies to build a fast counting device," writes biographer Robert Slater in *Portraits in Silicon*. Mauchly planned to use vacuum tubes, sealed shells used in audio amplifiers to control the flow of electricity. "While others thought Mauchly's plans were unrealistic, Eckert convinced him that his dream of building an electronic vacuum-tube computer was possible," Slater writes.

During World War II, the pair got an Army contract to develop a machine for calculating weapons-firing trajectories. The war finished before they did, but their creation—the first digital computer—proved them capable computer makers. In 1947, they founded their own company, which the Bureau of the Census hired to build a machine to handle its many chores of calculation.

Feeding the beast: making the UNIVAC go.

They nearly didn't do it; they ran out of cash. In 1950, Remington Rand, which made electric shavers and office machines, bought Eckert and Mauchly out, but kept them on the job. In '51, at a price of $159,000, Remington Rand handed the Census Bureau the Universal Automatic Computer—UNIVAC I, the world's fastest computer (at the time) and the first computer in America built for commercial sale.

UNIVAC was useful but not famous until 1952, when it predicted the outcome of the presidential election on CBS-TV. From then on, UNIVAC meant computer in the American mind. Remington Rand (which merged with Sperry Corporation in 1955) sold 46 UNIVAC Is during the 1950s, each for well into six figures. UNIVAC even scared the biggest office-machine company. "The popularity of UNIVAC was making IBM nervous; it had nothing to match Sperry's machine," says Slater.

Sperry retired UNIVAC I in 1957 and developed new UNIVACs, but IBM was moving up fast. IBM built better machines than UNIVAC; it focused on office machines, while Sperry handled all sorts of gadgets; its sales force outhustled Sperry's. In the 1960s, IBM meant computer in the American mind. The Census Bureau donated the original UNIVAC I to the Smithsonian Institution.

In the 1980s, Sperry was bought out by another machine maker, Burroughs, and stopped using the name UNIVAC. Only the company's current name, Unisys, even mildly suggests the mighty machine that changed American business and politics.

Floppy discs

Ah, the old days, when floppy discs were really floppy.

Those days began in 1971. Software developer Alan Shugart developed a round floppy disk for one of IBM's big mainframe computers. Discs were nothing new; computers had used hard discs since the 1950s, when they replaced reels of magnetic tape. (Discs could store more data than tape and didn't need rewinding.)

Shugart's innovation, the floppy, was eight inches wide, compared to the hard disc's 14. Made of the same flexible material as tape, floppies were lighter in weight than the metal hard discs, more portable, cheaper, and more easily moved from one disc drive to another. Thus they were perfect to transfer information from one computer to another or simply to store data or programs that didn't need permanent storage in any one computer.

Soon, Shugart was developing disc drives at his own company, Shugart & Associates. Software engineer Gary Kildall visited Shugart, saw his drives, and developed the Control Program for Microcomputers (CP/M), which could link a small computer's disc drives to the processors that ran its hard drive. (Controllers had existed in the past, but mostly for huge mainframe machines.)

After trying various media for storing CP/M data, Kildall chose floppy discs. Among the first buyers of CP/M were the members of the Homebrew Computer Club—the birthplace of Apple Computer.

Shugart was busy, too. Soon, he developed a floppy in a square envelope. The new disc could store more data than the eight-inch discs—and at 5¼ inches wide, about the size of a bar napkin, the new disc was ideal for personal computers, which ran small.

In 1978, when Apple introduced the Apple II personal computer and Tandy Radio Shack launched its TRS-80, both companies used the new floppy. The market for floppies grew to $1.6 billion by 1984.

It wouldn't grow much bigger. By 1982, techno-powerhouse Sony had developed a 3½-inch disc that could carry even more data than the five-incher. A hard, plastic cover surrounded the disc, making it more durable than the vulnerable floppy. The floppy's cover had a hole through which a computer could read the disc's data—or on which a clumsy typist could spill a drink, possibly ruining the disc; while Sony's disc cover had its own hole, it also had a little gate to protect the disc until the computer needed it.

Apple used the small, non-floppy disc in its new Macintosh computers. IBM and its clones soon followed. Within a few years, the floppy was obsolete. The smaller, harder disc was the industry standard.

Ah, the old days—when software really was soft.

Apple II computer

1976. Young computer fiends Steve Wozniak and Steve Jobs create the first Apple computer, the Apple I.

1977. They refine the Apple I and market it as the Apple II. The user-friendly machine has sales of $770,000.

1978. Sales grow to $7.9 million.

1979. Dan Bricklin, Bob Frankston, and Dan Fylstra create and market VisiCalc. The program, written on a II, is "a dynamic spreadsheet program that turned the Apple II into a powerful tool for forecasting economic results," according to *West of Eden: The End of*

The Apple II (specifically, the Apple IIc) at work.

Innocence at Apple Computer by technology journalist Frank Rose. He adds, "VisiCalc was the program that ushered the personal computer into the American office."

Apple II sales rise to $49 million. The II, says Rose, becomes "the most successful personal computer ever sold [up to that time]" and "a workhorse that gave rise to a whole industry."

1980. Software programmer Ken Williams, working on an Apple II with story and art by his wife, Roberta, creates Mystery House, the first high-resolution illustrated adventure game. Their two-person company, Sierra On-Line, has sales of $167,000 in its first year; three years later, it earns $10 million and has 93 employees.

1981. By now, more than 300,000 Apple IIs have been distributed. But danger lurks: IBM introduces its PC.

1982. Sales of Apple IIs hit $600 million. The Apple II is the best-selling personal computer in the business.

1983. Apple is still promoting the Apple II—a new version, the IIc, receives more than 50,000 orders as soon as it's introduced—but, says Rose, the II in any configuration is starting to become "an obsolete machine whose appeal seemed likely to dissipate at any moment."

Why? *MacUser* magazine's John C. Dvorak notes that Apple never improves the II's microprocessor—the chip that makes it go—even as the competition improves theirs. Consequently, IBM, its clones, and their software cut into the II's business. "Once spreadsheet programs [like VisiCalc] appeared on more-serious computers...businesspeople bailed from the Apple II," Dvorak explains.

1984. The two millionth Apple II is sold. Apple introduces the Macintosh, which can do all that the II can, and more. Says Dvorak, "The Apple II was marked for death the day the Mac was introduced."

1985–1993. Apple concentrates more and more resources on Macintosh and less on the II. IBM and other companies upgrade their computers to compete with the Mac, leaving the II nearly forgotten.

1994. In the 10th year of the Macintosh, Apple discontinues the Apple II.

COMMUNICATING AND RECORD KEEPING
Candlestick telephones

The classic candlestick phone.

Early phones were like early cars: fancy toys for the rich. There were art nouveau phones with swirly carvings; phones in voluptuous hourglass shapes; phones shaped like ancient Greek urns, complete with detailed carvings; and more. They were made of bronze or other costly metals.

The first private phone was installed in 1877. By 1900, more than 1,300,000 were in service. All households and businesses wanted phones. A phone designed so simply that a factory could cheaply and quickly mass-produce it would make a lot of money.

Western Electric took the bait. The manufacturer developed a brass tube on an unadorned, round base, "about the size and shape of a candle in a holder; hence the name candlestick," writes phone expert Ralph Meyer in *Old-Time Telephones!: Technology, Restoration and Repair.*

Western Electric launched the phone in 1904. Its metal pieces weren't bronze, but brass plated with nickel. To make a call, a person picked up the receiver and asked the local exchange to connect him. "It was destined to remain in use for over half a century and to become one of the most popular telephones of all time," write P.J. Povey and R.A.J. Earl in *Vintage Telephones of the World.* By 1907, more than nine million phones were in use, many of them candlesticks.

A threat to the candlestick hit the United States in the late 1920s: the handset desk stand, which American men called the French phone because many of them had first seen it while in France during World War I. While the candlestick's mouthpiece was mounted atop the tall, thin tube, with the earpiece attached by wire to the base, the handset phone mounted earpiece and mouthpiece in one unit (the handset), a setup that prevails today. The handset rested on a cradle or hook atop the base.

"When it was made available to the public, the favorable response was beyond expectation," *Vintage Telephones* says. "Northwest Bell, for example, anticipated orders for 3,000 [handset] instruments during the first year. In the event, 10,000 orders were received."

The candlestick didn't quit. Customers kept buying them, and at least one manufacturer (Stromberg-Carlson) was making them into the 1940s.

But the handset didn't quit, either. It dominated the phone business. By the 1960s, the candlestick had been extinguished.

Plug-in switchboards

Being a switchboard operator required sharp eyes to see which of a thousand or more holes in a switchboard fit particular phone numbers. It required fast reflexes to connect call after call. It required steely concentration to connect one call while three others buzzed, demanding connection. And it required bulletproof good cheer to handle hundreds of callers, all of whom wanted to be connected immediately.

That receptionists and telephone operators handled these demands at low pay and less respect is a tribute to hard work. It began on May 17, 1877, at 342 Washington Street in Boston. At that site, report Joseph Nathan Kane, Steven Anzovin, and Janet Podell in *Famous First Facts*, "Edwin Thomas Holmes was operating an electrical burglar-alarm business. Holmes' office was connected by wire to a number of banks and similar institutions, and the telephones were placed in the offices of a few of his subscribers and connected to these wires. The first switchboard was connected with the telephones on six subscribers when the service began."

A typical day at the switchboard.

The first public telephone exchange was opened in 1878, in New Haven, Connecticut. More opened soon, and switchboard operators, known as "hello girls," became an American constant.

As more and more homes and businesses added more and more phones, the Bell System added more and more switchboards. Large businesses opened their own. But the switchboards were "expensive, slow, and took up a lot of physical space and electrical power," write Constance Raymond Kraus and Alfred Duerig in *The Rape of Ma Bell: The Criminal Wrecking of the Best Telephone System in the World*.

The birth of dial phones in the 1920s was the start of the end for plug-in switchboards. Dialing a phone number connected the caller electronically, without anyone pushing or pulling a plug. Plug-in switchboards remained the norm, but the potential for change was in place.

Bell developed electronic switching and "stored program control"—an electronic memory "which could be easily altered [and] held the instructions for interconnecting calls rather than the masses of wires and relays used in older systems," Kraus and Duerig say. After a decade of research and development, and an investment of more than $500 million, the first electronic central office switchboard went to work in 1965.

Slowly, the old system started to fall apart. There were new names for new set-ups—PBX, Centrex, Audix—but the bottom line was that businesses, including phone companies, no longer needed banks of "hello girls" to connect callers.

Hello, Central? Thanks for all the good work.

Stock tickers and ticker tape

Paul Newman and stock ticker: *The Hudsucker Proxy*, **set in 1958.**

Under a bell jar it sat, clicking along, spitting out a paper strip that could send rich men leaping out skyscraper windows in suicidal despair. The paper itself sometimes got hurled out those same windows to celebrate heroes riding down New York's streets.

The stock ticker started with the telegraph, which Samuel Morse invented in 1832. "By 1856, when Western Union was founded, out-of-towners could place orders to buy and sell securities on Wall Street [by telegraph]," wrote historian Robert Sobel in *Inside Wall Street: Continuity and Change in the Financial District*. "Still, the telegraph did not create much in the way of new business for the New York brokers. An out-of-towner would have to know exactly what he wanted to buy or sell prior to using the telegraph.... Western Union and other telegraph companies understood this, and soon were working on a 'continuous telegraph' which would print current stock prices."

New York Gold Exchange vice president S.S. Laws invented a ticker in 1866. "The simple machine printed the selling prices for [gold] on a continuous basis," says Sobel. Other inventors perfected their own tickers. One such machine was Thomas Edison's first major invention; yet another inventor, E.A. Calahan, gave the ticker its name. Soon stock tickers clattered away in hundreds of brokerages, banks, and financial firms.

Used ticker tape had to be disposed of. New Yorkers found a way. "The earliest recording of a spontaneous tossing of ticker tape from building windows occurred on October 28, 1886, when Wall Street revelers celebrated the dedication of the Statue of Liberty," reports historian Charles Panati in *Panati's Parade of Fads, Follies and Manias*. "The first official [ticker-tape] parade was held in 1910 in honor of Teddy Roosevelt.... The parade route, a mile-long stretch up Broadway from Battery Park to City Hall, between skyscrapers, became known as the Canyon of

Heroes." Other parades followed: for aviator Charles Lindbergh in the 1920s; General Dwight Eisenhower in 1945; astronauts John Glenn in 1962 and Neil Armstrong, Michael Collins, and Buzz Aldrin in 1969; the New York Mets in 1969; and American hostages freed from Iran in 1981.

By '81, however, computer programs were replacing the ticker. When South African leader Nelson Mandela paraded down the Canyon of Heroes in 1990, ticker tape was so scarce that New York had to buy 150 miles of ticker tape–style paper ribbon to throw.

"Ticker-tape parades," says Panati, "are a uniquely American phenomenon." Appropriately so, since Americans invented the ticker machine.

Manual typewriter

It's an image out of old movies: the newsroom full of hard-bitten newsmen, fedoras askew, dead cigars poking from their mouths. Our hero, a gutsy reporter with a hot scoop, is pounding two fingers on a clattering Underwood. With every smack of a finger on a key and a type bar on the page, the carriage jerks to the right. Its bell dings, signaling that the reporter has reached the page's right margin. With a sweeping flourish, the reporter slams the carriage back to the left and finishes his story. Jumping out of his chair, he grasps the top of the page and yanks it from the machine. Clutching the page, he scrambles past his colleagues to the office of his cantankerous editor.

You don't get that kind of excitement from e-mailing.

It took a century of experimentation by various hands before Milwaukee publisher and printer Christopher Sholes invented the first workable typewriter in the late 1860s. By the mid-1870s, Sholes and his partners had a machine on the market, selling at $125.

The machine was named the Remington No. 1 after the gun makers who built them for Sholes. Mark Twain bought one and claimed later to be the first author to give a publisher a typed manuscript, for *Life on the Mississippi*.

The typewriter didn't grab America instantly, but once it did, it didn't let

The face that launched a thousand letters.

go. "By 1910, two million typewriters were in use in America," write Susan Jonas and Marilyn Nissenson in *Going, Going, Gone: Vanishing Americana.*

The manual typewriter began dying in the 1930s with the birth of the electric. Typists found that after they used an electric, a manual typewriter required heavy pounding. (At least, it felt like pounding.) "By 1954, over half of all typewriters in use were electric," write Jonas and Nissenson.

When computers came into every office, school, and home, the manual typewriter's doom was complete. Make a mistake? Don't mess around with Wite-Out; just backspace. Worried about the letter "o" filling in? Not with a PC. Is your roommate refusing to let you write a last-minute term paper because the rapping of type bars is keeping her awake? No problem with the quieter clicks of fingers on a computer keyboard or the soft hum of a printer.

In 1995, Smith-Corona, the last large manual typewriter maker in America, filed for bankruptcy protection. The era of the manual typewriter was over.

Carbon paper

When stock in Xerox (then called Haloid) first went on the market, some wealthy potential investors ignored it. After all, why buy into a company that made copiers as long as the world has carbon paper?

There it is: a carbon copy.

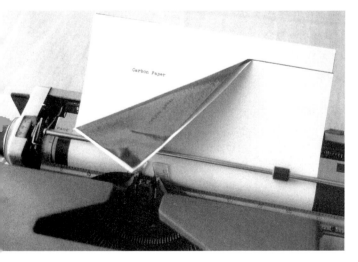

If these aloof plutocrats had spoken to their secretaries, though, they might have thought twice. For secretaries, carbon paper was at once a miracle and a nuisance.

Napoleon Bonaparte is said to have dismissed the English as "a nation of shopkeepers" (before Wellington knocked his lights out at Waterloo). England was indeed devoted to business. Its enterprises were spending plenty of expensive man-hours copying documents by hand. Anyone who could create a faster, cheaper way to copy could get rich.

In 1806, inventor Ralph Wedgewood did it. He soaked paper in ink and let it dry. He laid an uninked page over the inked one and another uninked page beneath it, and wrote on the top page. Voilà—the pressure from his writing pushed ink from the middle page onto the bottom one, producing an image identical to that on the top. Wedgewood reportedly started selling his invention out of a London shop and made a fine living.

Carbon paper entered every business office. It came in black, red, yellow, green, blue, brown, and even white. The bottom of business letters often displayed the cryptic reference "cc:" followed by a person's name; that person was to receive a carbon copy of the letter.

But carbons were a pain. "They were too black or too light, they were full of smudges, or they were hard to read," report Susan Jonas and Marilyn Nissenson in *Going, Going, Gone: Vanishing Americana*. "The carbon paper itself wrinkled easily, it curled, it tore."

Starting in the 1950s, xerography made carbon paper obsolete. By the end of the 1970s, an office that regularly used carbons was hard to find. And although "cc:" is still found on business correspondence, the senders are not thinking of carbon—the copy will be generated by a Xerox machine or a laser printer, or even sent via e-mail.

Receipt books and credit-card blanks still use carbons, but probably not for long. "Someone might steal the credit-card numbers imprinted on [the carbons]. Credit-card companies are replacing carbon sets with carbonless paper," say Jonas and Nissenson. "By the year 2000...the phrase 'She's a carbon copy of her mother' may need explaining."

all gone

Chapter Fifteen
SPORTS

Olympic athletes no longer compete in the 10,000-meter walk; that event hasn't been held since 1952. And the 80-meter hurdles vanished after 1968. Roller derby, which, at its peak in popularity in the early '70s, drew millions of fans to arenas and topped Nielsen TV ratings, is hard to find now. But most sports don't go away. As football grew popular, columnists imagined the demise of baseball and its slow, non-violent play, only to see baseball's popularity hold strong.

While entire sports don't usually vanish, aspects of them do. Stadiums, though huge and made of concrete, aren't as permanent as they look. In 1991, for example, the Chicago White Sox organization abandoned one of the country's most venerable diamonds, 81-year-old Comiskey Park, and replaced it with New Comiskey Park.

Even if stadiums remain in place, sometimes their teams don't. The Boston Braves became the Milwaukee Braves and then the Atlanta Braves. The Oakland Raiders moved to Los Angeles and then back to Oakland. Sometimes, a switch in location without a switch in names can get silly, as when New Orleans' basketball team moved to Salt Lake City, creating the nearly oxymoronic Utah Jazz.

Entire leagues can disappear, too. The American Football League—home of the Raiders, the New York Jets, and the New England Patriots—competed with the National Football League until getting merged into it. The National Basketball League put teams on the courts until it, too, became a part of the organization that would be called the NBA.

Finally, equipment can change. Football helmets without face guards belong to yesterday. Bare-knuckle pro boxing is out, replaced by gloved fights. White tennis balls, which were hard to follow on television, were dropped in favor of more videogenic neon-yellow balls. And unrehearsed pro wrestling matches—were there ever any in the first place?

Never mind. Let the games begin.

Ebbets Field and the Brooklyn Dodgers

In 1980, when the Baseball Hall of Fame inducted Dodger Duke Snider, he talked about a time when he and his tough, irreverent teammates cried. "We wept," he said, when his team left Brooklyn's Ebbets Field. "When they tore down Ebbets Field, they tore down a little piece of me."

The diamond from the air.

Ebbets Field has induced that sentiment in a lot of people. Bob Cooke, former sports editor of the *New York Herald Tribune*, wrote in 1981, "Ebbets Field…had broad concrete arms that would wrap themselves endearingly around the Dodger fans. Ebbets Field had a knack of sustaining a rookie's stumbling feet. It had a way of sheltering life." Journalist William Taaffe wrote in *Sports Illustrated*, "It was the warmest place, other than home, I have ever been."

Dodgers owner Charles Ebbets built his field in 1913 for $750,000. In the book *Pay Dirt: The Business of Professional Team Sports*, economists James Quirk and Rodney Fort note, "The cost of building Ebbets Field was so great that Charles Ebbets was forced to sell half the team."

Ebbets died in 1925. The surviving co-owners "couldn't stand each other," Quirk and Fort say. The enmity made running the team virtually impossible. "By 1938, the Dodgers were head over heels in debt."

Within a decade, team lawyer Walter O'Malley took control and part ownership of the team. The Dodgers entered a golden age.

The team had done well before—it was the National League champion in 1916, 1920, and 1941—but its run from '47 through '56 immortalized it. The

Dodgers played in six World Series, winning in 1955. Jackie Robinson, Don Newcombe, and Roy Campanella won Most Valuable Player awards. Robinson, Snider, and Carl Furillo set hitting records. Newcombe won the Cy Young pitching award. Newcombe, Joe Black, and Jim Gilliam won Rookie of the Year.

And Ebbets Field remained homey. "The stands were so close to the field, you could hear the Dodgers chatting," Taaffe remembers. In *Diamonds: The Evolution of the Ballpark*, Michael Gershman writes, "The gate in deep right-center was still opened after every game so that the fans could walk on the same grass as their heroes." Yearly attendance regularly topped a million—not bad for a park that seated 31,497.

But not good, either. O'Malley considered the park too small to make much profit. In 1958, the Dodgers moved to Los Angeles. In 1960, Ebbets Field was razed to make room for a public housing project. By 1997, a sign hung where second base once sat: NO BALL PLAYING.

Fortunately for the heritage of Ebbets Field, children nearby ignored the sign and played ball anyway.

Syracuse Nationals

In the early days of the National Basketball Association, some great teams made it to the championships: the Lakers, the Knicks, the Warriors, the Nats....

The who?

The Syracuse Nationals. In the team's 14 seasons, it reached the finals three times and once went all the way to victory. And its boss revolutionized the game.

Bowling-alley owner Danny Biasone founded the Nats in 1946 as part of the new National Basketball League. A competing group, the Basketball Association of America, took over the NBL in 1949 and changed the combined setup's name to the National Basketball Association.

The Nationals were one of the NBA's strongest teams. They had All-Star forward Dolph Schayes, a six-foot-eight future Hall of Famer specializing in rebounds. The team had player-turned-coach Al Cervi, one of the NBA's toughest leaders, "who would pound one of his players in a one-on-one clinic to prove a point," reported sportswriter Roland Lazenby in *The NBA Finals: The Official Illustrated History*. Four of Cervi's players—Schayes, Fuzzy Levane, Alex Hannum, and Paul

Seymour—became NBA coaches themselves. With such talent, the Nats reached the NBA finals in 1950, '54, and '55, taking the championship in '55.

But early basketball had a problem: it was a game of stalls and fouls. Boston Celtics player Bob Cousy said, "The team in front [in points] would hold the ball indefinitely...nobody dared take a shot, and the game slowed up." He added, "The only way you could get [the ball] was by fouling." The Celtics hit Schayes so hard that they broke his wrist. The Lakers did the same to Nats guard George King. Forward Earl Lloyd suffered a fractured hand. "The press took to calling us the 'bandage brigade,'" Schayes said.

So Biasone created the "shot clock." A team now had to shoot within 24 seconds of getting the ball. "The 24-second shot clock made its debut on October 30, 1954, and its effect was immediate," reports sportswriter Alex Sachare in *The Official NBA Encyclopedia*. The game sped up, scores rose, and fouls decreased.

Celtics president Red Auerbach called the shot clock "the single most important rule change in the last 50 years." "Without the clock, I think the pro game definitely would have disappeared," Schayes said. "Biasone saved the NBA," said Fort Wayne Pistons coach Charlie Eckman.

Unfortunately, he didn't save his own team. After the '55 season, the Syracuse Nationals never again reached the finals. In 1963, the team left town; its name was changed to the Philadelphia 76ers.

The 76ers became one of the modern NBA's strongest teams. It's a nice legacy for one of the early NBA's finest.

The Negro Leagues

"On September 28, 1860, the Weeksville of New York engaged the Colored Union Club," reports sportswriter Mark Ribowsky in *A Complete History of the Negro Leagues: 1884 to 1955*. That baseball game between two African-American teams inaugurated organized Black baseball in the United States. (Weeksville won 11-0.)

By 1867, several Black teams were scheduling games against each other. Their first official league, the Southern League of Base Ballists, was born in the late 1880s. The National Colored Base Ball League soon followed.

The leagues eventually collapsed. As sportswriter Bruce Chadwick says in *When the Game Was Black and White: The Illustrated History of the Negro Leagues*,

"Most black clubs during the era from 1900 to 1919 never had a league, or a semblance of one, that lasted more than a single season."

In 1920, Chicago American Giants manager Andrew "Rube" Foster changed all that. He gathered the Black teams' owners in Kansas City to set up the Negro National League.

The new leagues were well run. In 1924, they played the first Black World Series, and in 1933, their first All-Star game. Bill "Bojangles" Robinson and Louis Armstrong owned teams. Players included Jackie Robinson, Hank Aaron, Willie Mays, Satchel Paige (who won, says Ribowsky, over two thousand games), and Josh Gibson (who for a while hit about 70 runs per season).

And the games were popular. A Negro League All-Star game drew 51,000 fans to Chicago's Comiskey Park, says Chadwick. "The New York Yankees," writes Ribowski, "were said to have earned around $100,000 a year on Negro League games at the mecca of Yankee Stadium."

In 1947, the Brooklyn Dodgers put Jackie Robinson in the game. As other teams added Black players, "it effectively killed the Negro Leagues," Chadwick says. "Fans didn't have to go to the [Negro League] games to see their heroes, so they didn't." One by one, Negro League teams died. The last one, the Kansas City Monarchs, quit in 1965.

The leagues' greats have received some honors, such as induction into the Baseball Hall of Fame and a hall of their own. "The Negro Leagues Baseball Museum...opened to the public in 1991 in a city steeped in Black baseball traditions—Kansas City," Randy Giancaterino, Paul Debono, and Barbara Gregorich wrote in the journal *American Visions*.

Wherever he is, Rube Foster is probably smiling.

The Washington Senators

In the musical *Damn Yankees*, the devil turns an aging baseball fan into a young ballplayer, partly because the devil didn't want those "damn Yankees" to win another World Series. The ballplayer joins the Washington Senators.

The Senators had a long history. Founded in 1892, the team was weak, finishing last in 1904. "It was a hardy breed of fans that the nation's capital had spawned. They had to be, or else they would have become extinct, the victims of heartbreak," writes sportswriter Shirley Povich in the 1959 anthology *The American League*. For managers, Povich adds, "Washington was the graveyard."

Starting in 1912, things changed. The team often finished first in its division, propelled early on by the pitching of Walter "Big Train" Johnson and always by the leadership of owner Clark Griffith. In 1924, '25, and '33, the Senators were in the World Series, winning in '24, with President Calvin Coolidge in the stands for the opener.

Nor did their glory end there. In 1957, Senator Roy Sievers led the league in home runs (42) and runs batted in (114). In 1962, pitcher Tom Cheney struck out 21 batters in a single game. "He set a record that has never been matched," Brad Herzog, author of the athlete-ranking tome *The Sports 100*, later wrote in *Sports Illustrated*.

Yet the Senators were inconsistent. They finished last in 1958.

Fans came and went, too. Senators manager Ted Williams said, "There was a hard core of fans here, all right, but there were only six or seven thousand of them. Basically, Washington is a city of transient people. Most people didn't give a damn." Things got so dire that the city sued the team for not paying rent on the city-owned stadium where it played.

In 1971, the ax fell. Owner Robert Short obtained permission from other American League owners to move his team to Dallas. President Nixon called the change "heartbreaking." Washington city council chairman Gilbert Hahn claimed that the city would invite the San Diego Padres or San Francisco Giants to move there, but neither team budged.

And so the Senators were gone. Still, they can't be forgotten. After all, no other team had among its hometown fans congressmen, Cabinet secretaries, genuine law-making senators, and the president of the United States.

The reserve clause

In the past, old-timers recall, a player stayed with his team a long time. The hometown heroes had loyalty, dadgummit.

Actually, no. They had the reserve clause, a part of every player's contract. "This fiat, instituted in 1879, decreed that a club reserved and retained the services of Player X in perpetuity—until he was washed up, retired, or peddled on the market," writes sportswriter Al Stump in *Cobb: A Biography*. The clause trapped baseball star

Ty Cobb with the Detroit Tigers for more than 20 years. He exhorted state legislatures and enlisted at least one U.S. senator to kill the clause. Nothing worked. He pulled free only when a scandal involving fixed ball games got him fired.

The clause hit other sports, too. ABC Sports president Roone Arledge said of O.J. Simpson, "He was the most sought-after college player of all time. He could have marketed his services for millions of dollars, and he wanted to play for Los Angeles. But instead, he went to Buffalo and took whatever [the Bills] felt like giving him, which wasn't much. He played on a lousy team with a lousy line for a coach who wouldn't let him carry the ball. It was only luck that, after years of frustration, Buffalo finally changed coaches and drafted some good linemen. Otherwise, O.J.'s entire career would have been ruined—by the reserve clause."

Others fought the clause as Cobb had, but they all lost—until October 7, 1969, when Curt Flood, a quiet center fielder whose hobby was portrait painting, refused to let the St. Louis Cardinals trade him to the Philadelphia Phillies. In January 1970, Flood, aided by the players' union, sued to kill the clause. He lost, but the union fought on, using the publicity of Flood's case to establish binding arbitration between players and owners. In 1975, the system allowed pitchers Dave McNally and Andy Messersmith to become free agents, a precedent that fatally wounded the reserve clause. Other players followed, bounding from team to team. Millionaires filled the playing fields.

It was too late for Cobb or Flood, though. The former was dead, the latter retired. But all athletes would agree to the words that Flood addressed to baseball commissioner Bowie Kuhn and that would stand as the reserve clause's epitaph: "I do not feel I am a piece of property to be bought and sold."

United States Football League

For a few years, the United States Football League flashed across sports pages and TV sets. Then it butted heads with the giant.

The league began strongly in the early 1980s. Among the first team owners was real estate emperor Donald Trump. His New Jersey Generals caused a tempest in 1983—before the USFL had played even one game—when they signed 20-year-old Heisman Trophy winner Herschel Walker in a deal that made him the highest-paid player in football.

Such expenses soon seemed justified: the USFL was gaining fans. The Jacksonville Bulls nearly sold out the 80,000-seat Gator Bowl. ABC signed a three-year, $34 million contract to televise USFL games. ESPN aired them, too. The league expanded, reaching 18 teams in 1984.

The players were thrilled. Birmingham Stallion Cliff Stoudt said, "For seven years, I was a backup in Pittsburgh [to quarterback Terry Bradshaw]. I wasn't sure I could be a starter. Now, I know I can."

The owners weren't so happy. They lost nearly $200 million by 1986 and projected losses of up to $5 million per team from then on. The normal start-up expenses of so large an operation and the high bidding for talent like Walker were killing them. In 1986, the league shrunk to eight teams.

That year the USFL, prodded by Trump, switched its playing season from spring to fall, directly opposite the NFL. ABC, planning to run NFL games, dropped its USFL contract. ESPN kept the league on cable, but no broadcast network picked it up.

Since the USFL couldn't survive without network TV revenue, the league sued the NFL for $1.69 billion, claiming that the NFL forced the networks to shut the USFL out. In July, a federal court ruled that the NFL did compete unfairly. Then it gave the USFL only one dollar in damages.

Herschel Walker of the Generals on the run.

Trump had had enough. At an owners' meeting a few days later, he pulled the Generals from the fall season. Tampa Bay Bandits owner Lee Scarfone said, "The ESPN television contract required that there be a New York area team. When [Trump] said no, it didn't matter how the rest [of the owners] voted." The USFL was dead.

Most players were out of work, but some picked up NFL jobs. Walker set records with the Philadelphia Eagles. The Los Angeles Express' Steve Young became a top quarterback on the San Francisco 49ers. Memphis Showboat Reggie White became an all-pro lineman on the Green Bay Packers. Doug Flutie, Jim Kelly, and Kelvin Bryant joined the NFL, too.

Walker recalled the league fondly. "The USFL was fun. It was what the NFL used to be. I'm not much for dancing, but I loved to watch the shimmies in the end zone, the high fives, the sack dances." Stoudt agreed: "The USFL gave to me what it gave everybody who played in it: so much confidence, excitement, freshness."

afterword

But what about ...

Hey, wait a minute! What about skate keys?

Or the Rochester Royals basketball team?

Or White Tower hamburgers? Fluoroscopes for fitting shoes? Penny postcards? Commodore Amiga computers? Van Dyke cigars? The Zuider Zee? The Frito Bandito? Break dancing?

What about all of the recently extinct animals: the Texas red wolf, Tecopa pupfish, dusky seaside sparrow, Amistad Gambusia fish?

The problem with writing a book like this is that there are too many topics to cover. If this book sells well enough to warrant a sequel—*All Gone Too: More Things That Aren't There Anymore*, perhaps—I'll try to cover them there.

I've had a good time dipping into the past. But it's sad to look back on all of the things that aren't there anymore. For now, it's time to look ahead.

I'll see you in the 21st century.

photo credits